Fantasy Football: Lessons

7 Valuable lessons that will make you a better Fantasy Football player

Lessons: 7 valuable lessons that will make you a better Fantasy Football player by Ken Kocon

Published by Majestic Mountain Publishing
Printed in the United States of America

ISBN 0-9768386-0-5

LCCN 2005925742

DISCLAIMER
Every effort has been made in completing this book to the accuracy of content. No responsibility is assumed for omissions, errors, inaccuracies or inconsistencies. This book is intended for informational entertainment purposes only. Any slight of organizations, players, people or places is unintentional. The author and publisher shall not be held liable for damage caused or alleged damage caused, indirectly or directly from text and websites contained in this book.

If you are not in agreement with the above disclaimers you can return the book to the publisher and will receive a full refund.

Graphic Design: Steve Blexrud
www.steveblexrud.com

Table of Contents

Foreword

Most people who compete in something have an innate drive to win. We all like the deep down feeling we get when we are finally number one at something.

Whether it is at work and your project is a huge success or standing up in front of our peers and receiving an accommodation. How do you feel when your son or daughter achieves a major life accomplishment? The excitement of when they perform in a school concert or play. The adrenaline high you feel if they play on the sports team and you attend the games. Those positive energies are something that we all enjoy.

I get that drive and feeling from being extremely good at Fantasy Football. To be good at something you must put in some time to study, read, and research. This does not necessarily mean that the person who spends the most time studying wins. No. Time is what you make of it. Realistically information becomes available at key times during the week if you can gather all your information and at one time go thru it, you can make a successful, intelligent weekly lineup. This would be the bare minimum requirements, but if you drafted well and the injury bug was hungry for a piece of someone else you have clear sailing.

Preface

Fantasy Football is a growing exciting sport in which 12 million Americans participate. It invigorates the competitive gene in both sports fans and non sports fans. Fantasy buffs even find meaning in those non playoff deciding NFL games.

More and more people are getting involved and in places were it is legal, it can be big money. Las Vegas has the World Championship of Fantasy Football where the winner walks away with $200,000.

You can also find leagues in local newspapers, the USA today and online. And yes some of these leagues, you can win money and prizes. If you have never played Fantasy Football before or are fairly new to the sport you want to read Lesson #6 first. How to play Fantasy Football.

This book is intended to help you find the edge in this growing sport whether online, or with your buddies playing for the big time. You might even learn a little about the game of Football itself.

Enjoy-Ken Kocon

Acknowledgements

I would like to thank all my buddies whom I have competed with and against over the years.

Thanks to my former roommates Todd and Sean who I spent many a late night watching games while discussing fantasy players, trades, and free agents.

Most recently Derek, Bryan, Kevin, Billy, Bobby, TC, T-Dog, Chris, Big Daddy, Arne, Dave and Rick.

My Mom, Dad, Karen, Russell, and David and their extended families for their love and support over the years.

And lastly to my best friend my wife Maria.

Lesson #1 What You Need to Look for in a Fantasy Football Magazine and Where to Gather Predraft Information.

The heat of summer is getting to you and you long for the crisp cool nights of fall. Baseball season is in full swing and if you play Fantasy Baseball you are all geared for the morning paper. The adrenaline is flowing as you are hoping for that CG 8 IP, 3 H, 10 K's, W, while your wolf down that second bowl of raisin bran. While you finish getting ready for work you might even catch the ticker line on ESPN Sports Center for more data input.

These little insignificant times where you can catch a glimpse here, a transaction there are huge in staying updated on the competition. While baseball season is going the sweet sounds of September are dancing in my head.

Start your pursuit of knowledge by reading the NFL notes and transaction page in your sports page everyday. As I am writing this, Mushin Muhammad has just left the Carolina Panthers and signed with the Bears. Carolina didn't want to pay

Muhsin the 10 million dollar roster bonus due on 3/2/05, so Chicago signed him and gave him a $12 million signing bonus guaranteed. I am sure Mushin was disgruntled employee for all of 2 days.

The other hot story of last week was Moss to Oakland for Napoleon Harris a LB and a 7th round pick. I live in purple country and this just continues our misery. However now that the curse of the Bambino is broken, can my four time Super Bowl losers (Vikings) finally break the "curse of the Whiskey bottle."

Let me take you back.... The year is 1975 and time is running out in the NFC title game between the Dallas Cowboys and the Minnesota Vikings. Minnesota is clinging to a 14-10 lead when Roger Staubach whips a 50 yard Hail Mary pass down the right sideline. There is contact and a yellow hankie streaks thru the crisp January air. Drew Pearson pushes Nate Wright to the ground and catches the pass for a touchdown, Dallas 16, Minnesota 14. Clearly the ref is calling Offense pass interference and the play will not stand. NOOO! Defensive pass interference is called by the referee. Touchdown Dallas. At that moment a whiskey bottle flies from the end zone bleachers and hit's the Zebra in the head. Thus the curse of the Whiskey bottle is born. The Vikes were 12-2 that year and clearly were one of their most dominating teams ever. It was their year. They have never won the Super Bowl. It is "the Curse of the Whiskey bottle."

Sorry to get sidetracked there. The point on the Mushin situation being that the NFL season is going on year long. There is ever changing Fantasy news that you could miss out on by not paying attention. At your league draft next year, someone in your league might actually say "give me Mushin from the Panthers".

As a glory seeker of the gridiron, you should immediately be thinking, how this affects their fantasy values. You should be thinking of not only those particular players' values but their quarterbacks, teammates, and former teams. Did their team turn from a running team into a passing team? Are they a new offensive juggernaut?

As for the answer to the previous questions I will say, the Raiders will tend to favor a vertical passing game. Because we all know that we cannot name the true number one back in Oakland. (Could be Lamont Jordan, pay attention in training camp) Collins is a serviceable Quarterback but as never thrown more than 22 TD's in a year. Porter is signed to a long term deal and makes a solid receiver on the other side. Moss's value is still high as he is an unbelievable talent and the grass should be better on his overall health. Moss will have 12-15 TD's if he plays a full schedule, still the cream of the crop at his position.

Culpepper's value drops a little at this point. However it still depends on if the Vikes pickup someone thru free agency or draft a stud, like a Brandon Edwards/Mike Williams. Daunte is unlikely to have the career year he had last year and I expect the Vikes to be less efficient in the Red Zone. More field goals will be the answer, if they can find a kicker who can kick past 40 yards.

Mushin's situation is precarious. The starting QB in Chicago is .... Umh, Rex Grossman is the answer, who hurt is coming of a knee injury but should be ready for camp. Chicago is extremely brutal on offense, but they do have a couple of things going for them. They play in the NFC a conference full of mediocrity (besides the Eagles). And they play one of the worst secondaries in the Green Bay Packers twice a year. I would expect Mushin to be in the 8-10 TD range.

Carolina will suffer in the passing game, however Colbert is showing he can perform at this level and makes a good sleeper. They relied on Mushin more because their number one receiver Steve Smith was out. Carolina's backfield also took a beating, with Foster and Davis gone for the year to injuries. I see them reverting more to Head

Coach Fox's style, ball control, run first team. I do think based on the way they finished up last year Carolina will be a good football team.

As you can see my preparation has already started. Reading the sports section, particularly the NFL notes, will keep you up to date on the latest big name information. You should try to read it everyday. However if you are busy with your careers and life in general, the best times to get high value with minimal time investment are: Right after free agency opens, typically the first couple of weeks in March. Right before the draft, which will be the 3rd or 4th weekend in April. And right after the draft to familiarize with the players drafted and any draft day trades. In the appendix II will discuss the 2005 rookie Crop.

As the season nears, training camp time is a must read time. You want to stay updated on the injuries and who is winning the starting positions battles.

Getting started seriously should start with the purchase of a couple of good solid fantasy football magazines. Get at least 2-3 publications to give yourself different perspectives.

One of my favorites is "Fantasy Football Pro Forecast." You might have to go to multiple stores and shop to get more than one magazine. You definitely will see one magazine in multiple places, typically the local gas station or grocery store. If you have a local draft this will be the one everyone has and to your advantage. You can also call your fantasy friends and ask them before the draft which magazine they have and where they got it. For regional appeal it will probably be the one with the local team player. Last year Ahman Green was on my favorite publication "Fantasy Football Pro Forecast". After purchasing the first magazine you need to shop for that second magazine which is different from the first.

Bookstores like Barnes and Noble tend to carry multiple magazines and will save you all the running around. You should have no problem finding something that has different information than the first and help cover all the key pieces of info that we will cover next.

When buying a magazine you will be paying $7 to $8 dollars per publication. Before you plunk down $16 on two magazines make sure you have the following areas covered:

PLAYER RANKINGS

Player rankings are standard in any fantasy magazine. The publication will generally rank the players by position: quarterback (QB), running back (RB), wider receiver (WR), tight end (TE), defense (D), and kicker (K).

I like the guides that start with a blurb about the position and then go on the talk about the different levels of players. I will define the different levels of player with the following designators, the *franchise player, the golden boys, the players with potential*; *you've got to be kidding me*, and the *no way in hell*. Obviously, the players are ranked from best to worst. Other magazines have formulas that give you a different insight. In some of these publications you will also find a panel of experts top 10 players at a position, a juicy little bonus.

Having two different pieces of literature on your players will give you some different viewpoints on certain players. This will help give a balanced look at who they feel are the top 10 players at their position. We will use this info later to help decipher our own list.

CHEAT SHEETS

Technically the cheat sheet is just another form of the player rankings. You want one that has the rankings by basic (Touchdown only) and combinational scoring. (TD and Yardage). The cheat sheet will have the top 100 to 200 players ranked overall regardless of position. You also want a cheat sheet with the top players ranked at the individual positions. QB's should have a list of at least 50, RB's 50-70, WR's 75-120, TE's 1-50, K's 1-32+, D's 1-32.

If you are looking at this and wondering about the QB's and Kickers numbers, you still have some rookies and undecided positions. Lack of a true starter is a dangerous area that will suck the life out of any team. We will discuss later in ranking your players.

YEAR END STATISTICS

Varying on the current player ranking list is last year's final player stats at their position. A quick reference to refresh your memory on Fantasy scoring statistics like, TD's, catches, 100 yd games, and yards. This is nice to have but can get off the internet if your magazine does not have a quick reference guide.

THE ROOKIES

The next critical piece of info is the rookie crop. There will be some player in this group that your fantasy buddies has already decided is the next Jerry Rice, Dan Marino or Barry Sanders. He will want this particular player and want him bad. The rookie probably will be drafted too high with a reach pick and leaving you with a sure thing.

The rookies will be listed by position and let

you know who the heck they are and how the magazine feels they fit it. Will these New Money Millionaires be impact players or busts? For a breakdown of the possible rookie impact players of 2005 visit the appendix of this book.

TEAM PROFILES

To help sort thru how rookies, free agents and individual players impact the Fantasy game, it is important to read individual team profiles. Make sure your magazine contains them. Read every one of them, not just your favorite teams, word for word.

Also pay attention to the coaching, does this team have a coach who is an offensive guru or a one dimensional 3 yard cloud of dust guy.

Check out the offensive line report. Do they have any gapping holes due to injuries, holdouts or retirements? A bad offensive line with no experience together can be the end of any consistent point production for a player.

How about free agents? Has this team signed anyone who will compete for playing time at key offensive positions?

On the defensive side have they done anything to improve? The Minnesota Vikings immediately come to mind with the signing of 2 new defensive free agents and trading for 2 starters.

SLEEPER LIST

The proverbial sleeper and bust list is always good to look at. I look at the lists and what the magazine has to say. Does this list agree with mine based on what constitutes sleeper.

MOCK DRAFT

Not every publication has this but a good mock draft will help answer a lot of your questions about who will go where in the draft. Make sure you read about the scoring rules the teams are drafting under and that yours are comparable. Sports weekly by USA will come out with a draft issue. Buy it. You also should be able to come up with a couple on the internet.

Good preparation includes asking other people about their draft. Make sure to ask: "Who went first?" "Where did Owens go?" Even ask about a couple of your sleepers. Make sure you ask specific questions. Depending on how many people you talk with, more is better, this will give you a good idea of how long you can sit on a player.

Team Dept Chart-These are listings of the projected players by position in order of starters. Preferably the AFC teams are on one page and the NFC is on the other.

Something in this format:

QB	1	WR1	1	K	1
	2		2		
RB	1		3		
	2	WR2	1		
	3		2		
	4		3		
FB	1	TE	1		
	2		2		

NFL SCHEDULE/STRENGTH OF SCHEDULE

Finally, the last section wraps it all together and will help give you that competitive edge in the playoffs. It really is quite simple. The NFL schedule.

Some publications will even provide a list based on winning percentage of who has the easiest schedule the coming year. They will rank the teams from easiest schedule to hardest based on the last years winning percentage of their opponents. This can be fairly useful however the hole is that teams get better and play better defense especially in the years of parity.

There are some websites that break down schedules further for the entire year. You want to particularly pay attention to who your players play in weeks 14, 15, 16 and 17. (Depending on your Championship week) By looking at match ups these weeks for your players you are planning ahead to win the Championship. This is different then just trying to make the playoffs and seeing what happens. This is important to consider when you are ranking your own players and will take a perennial playoff contender owner, to a title winner. When the season is on the line wouldn't you love to have your studs lined up at home against the crème puffs of the league. Start clearing the mantel for the hardware baby!

OTHER INFORMATION SOURCES

To round out your predraft scouting you should read up on the internet all the latest insight. There are many websites that will have some feature articles and you should be able to get a current injury report.

Appendix III provides some websites that are very solid in giving you profiles and updates. Before the draft these sites will probably have a link to a cheat sheet too and a latest sleeper, bust list that will add to the plethora of knowledge you have acquired.

As talked about earlier Sports Weekly by USA Today comes out with a publication weekly on Wednesday's. This is a good source of data to have before the draft and weekly. They do their draft early enough where you can get your hands on another mock draft. I recommend highly reading the draft issue of this publication and have it available on draft day.

Lesson #2 Interpreting the Information to Develop Your Own Player Rankings

Now we are ready to crunch all the info we have gathered to develop our own personal player rankings. I mean this literally. We will not be drafting off of a cheat sheet like everyone else. This will be our first advantage and edge that we have gained on a number of people.

Do me a favor, when you get to your local draft look at how many people bring their own magazines? Now look at the cover of the magazines? How many of these are the same?

Ideally one of your publications is the same magazine so you are looking at the same info as everyone else and the same cheat sheet. Some people will literally go right down the list provided on the cheat sheet as players are drafted and crossed off. It is very predictable and … your advantage.

Cyber drafts you can find the same thing. Obviously you can't see everyone's magazine but you can ask them if they show up early. To keep from making it obvious you can ask them who is on the cover of their magazine. Who is that by? A lot of times the player on the cover will be based on region but the info is the same.

In the online draft rooms I've experienced the cheat sheet comes up in your live draft room in a little box with the next highest ranked group of players. Predictably, some owners will go in order based on position of need. If owners are not present this will be how the computer assigns them to that owner. There should be a que where you can bring up everyone's roster and predict where they are going. (Use it early on and it will become clear who did their research, who is letting the computer pick, and who is just picking in order.)

If you have never played Fantasy Football skip ahead to Lesson #6 and read the entire chapter on How to play Fantasy football.

We are now ready to prepare our personal rankings. Before you sit down to do this you should have the following materials in front of you:

Your leagues rules and scoring.

The book Lesson's

A pen

A spiral notebook

2 to 3 Fantasy Magazines

Sports Weekly by USA today

Any online materials like, sleepers, injury report, and the latest team depth charts.

I personally like to start with the question: If I get the number one pick, who would I take? Figure it out yet? Peyton Manning with his 49 TD strikes would be hard to top. Odds are against him throwing that many again however all the key people on offense should be back and to toss 40 is easily within reach.

Under the running back theory, any starting KC running back that runs behind that gifted line should get solid consideration. Wow what a group, in-between Mr. Holmes, L Johnson, and Blaylock (NY Jets now) they amassed 31 TD's. The key is finding out if Priest is the man when he comes back at 31 years old and a bad knee. The second closest running back last year was Shaun Alexander at 16.

It really would depend on your leagues scoring on QB touchdowns. Are passing touchdowns 3 pts, 4 pts, or 6 pts. For argument sake at 3 points x 40 TD's, Manning has 120 pts. If Priest runs for 20 at 6 per TD, we also have 120 pts. We have counted Priest out before and he keeps hanging hardware on the mantel. I don't think you could go wrong on either angle if Priest is healthy.

Just to make things interesting I am going to go against the running back theory that you hear about, and read about. I take Manning.

Now that I have finished that exercise, I will begin ranking my Quarterbacks.

I will make a list down the left had side of my page at the red margin line. I will go 1 thru 24 since I will not take more then 2 QB's in a draft. I have Peyton listed number one, McNabb is number 2 and then list them all the way down to number 24.

STRATEGY: A Franchise QB and his #1 Receiver will pay off big.

QUARTERBACKS

When ranking a quarterback you want to be looking at the following criteria

1. Are they the clear cut number 1 starter? Do not draft someone as your starting quarterback and hope he gets the job. Good Quarterbacks throws one to two TD's consistently every week. Draft a solid entrenched QB that you don't have to worry about getting yanked every week. Many theories are you can win with a late round QB pick. You can put you have to get a good consistent one. Top running backs don't even average a touchdown a week. A Quarterback will provide that offense. You need to score points consistently not have 80 pts one week and 20 points the next. 40 pts consistently (depending on your scoring system) every week will win you more games.

2. What is his average TD passes over the last 2 to 3 years? Has he thrown over 20, 25, 26-29,

30+? There is only one Quarterback who has throw over 30 TD's the last 2 years and no one has done it for 3 yrs. Mr. Brett Farve. Consistency baby got to love it. With the new enforcement of the no contact, I expect TD passes to rise. Over the next few years I expect 30 TDs to be more common. Four quarterbacks threw over 30 TDs last year. Five were between 26 and 29. Keep in mind your running quarterbacks can be worth 2-4 TD's a year. Michael Vick is the obvious one and Culpepper might be inclined to run more without Moss.

3. What kind of offense do they run? Do they run a 3 wide out, one back set (St Louis and Minn)? Do they have the stud running back and no wide receivers that lends to the ground game (Jets and Dallas). Do they have a great defense and are intending on playing the field position game. (Baltimore)

4. Who are they throwing to? 11 receivers caught over 10 TD passes and 5 more caught over 9 TD's. Donavan McNabb showed last year what a good wide out can do for you offense. Remember when drafting a QB make sure they have a decent receiver. Tom Brady is the only exception and with the trade of Patten I expect Branches numbers to go up.

5. What kind of shape is their offensive line in? A QB who is picking his teeth out of his mouth

guard is having a hard time making reads. When you did your predraft information gathering did you check thoroughly the offensive line report. Experienced lines with depth are a big bonus. Injuries will happen and the QB needs time to hit the deeper throws that result in the longer TD's.

6. What do the magazines have to say and what is their reasoning? They have their arguments and can be quite persuasive. Sort through what they say and give some weight to where they have them ranked.

7. How good will their team be? Teams that win consistently keep their formula the same. If teams start losing and falling out of the races they begin to experiment and start playing for next year. For instance your team is out of the playoff hunt and your Quarterback is in the last year of his contract. We have a stud rookie on our bench, and I don't know if Joe QB fits into our plans next year. Unless the QB is having an MVP year this could be a huge problem come playoff time.

8. Who is their coach and what kind of offense do they favor? Is this a run first or pass first offense. Mike Martz (St Louis Rams) is notorious for throw first. Herman Edwards will run constantly and play a more conservative style. Mike Holmgren loves to throw in Seattle however when you have 2 receivers who have problems

catching the ball and Shawn Alexander. Handing the ball off to your running back makes obvious sense.

For quarterback jobs that are undecided, rank the players on the same line together and put a slash in between them.

Example: We are at our 22nd QB ranking. Bledsoe/Testaverde Dallas. Next at 23. Frerotte/Feeley Miami. Notice these are well down on the list and I would have drafted my two quarterbacks before then. However, you will keep this list for referral during season long free agency.

PLAYER CLASSIFICATIONS

After completing your rankings you are going to look at your list and divide them into the terms we had discussed earlier. The *franchises players, golden boys, players with potential, you've got to be kidding me,* and the rest. What you are going to do is literally draw a line dividing the groups.

Example:

1. Manning — Franchise players
2. McNabb

----

3. Culpepper — Golden boys
4. Farve
5. Brady
6. Vick

7. Green
8. Brees

This is a hypothetical example. Manning and McNabb should throw over 30 TD's again this year making them 1st round picks. There will probably be a good number of interchangeable *golden boys* after that who will throw in that 25-30 TD range.
Mark the next level, the players with potential and so on until all levels are defined in your ranks. You will have 4 or 5 groups being that you won't need to rank the bottom dwellers unless you are considering drafting more then 2 QB's or take an injured player.

RUNNING BACKS
Now that we have drafted our signal caller let's move on to the stable and look at the thoroughbreds. You basically are going to repeat the same process with different criteria. Make a list for your RB's; however your running back list will be longer. You will probably want to rank at least 30-40. If you are in a 12 team league and everybody drafted 4-5 that would be 48-60. Having a good solid 30-40 on your list will give you a good crop of players to add some depth to a high injury position.

STRATEGY-Draft 5 running backs if the league

rules and roster limits allow you. With a 14-15 player roster this shouldn't be a problem. This will Give you much needed depth for injuries and byes. In addition it will give you a very marketable area of strength with which to trade.

Here are the criteria to look at when ranking your running backs.

1. Are they the only horse in the stable? Are they the number 1 starter? Last year it was opening weekend and I was watching Pittsburgh muscle Oakland up and down the field with Duce Staley in the running game. However when they got close to the goal line out trotted "The Bus", Jerome Bettis for the one yard TD plunge. TOUCHDOWN. Bettis final line was 3 carries, 1 yd 3 TD's, 18 pts. I was in tears laughing at all the poor people who drafted Staley. Be aware of any team that splits carries. These players should be drafted later as backups.

2. What was their average rushing TD's over the last two years? Was it 10, 12, 14, over 15? These are signs of consistency in both the player and just as important the offensive philosophy. When they get close to the goal line, they have faith in their number 1 stud to pound it in.

3. Is he a goal line guy or is there a goal line vulture that will prey on the easy one yard plunges. Barry Sanders was subject to this late in his career.

Also, refer to Bettis story above.

4. Is the offensive line intact? Injuries, free agent departures and lack of experience can really hurt a running back in his yards per carry and impact on the field. You can use the old saying of who was the better back, Barry Sanders or Emmitt Smith. The argument is behind Emmitts Offensive line you could get 100 yds and a score consistently. The new consistently dominating lines in football now are KC, 31 TD's by their backs, SD, and Denver. Look at last years list of top rushers and some teams have more then one.

5. Will his team score a lot of points? Specifically will they score touchdowns? A team that has a brutal red zone attack is going to turn your face three shades of red when they continually have to settle for a field goal. These will be the 800-1000 yard backs with 6, 7, or 8 TD's. Their team's fails to consistently put them in a position for the 1-yard plunge, and these backs lack the speed to take it to the house from farther out.

6. Is he in a running offense or passing? The more touches your player gets the more chances he has to score.

7. What does the fantasy magazine say? The publication will have some well thought out insight to help you shape your rankings.

Separate the *franchise players* from the *golden boys* with a line and so on all the way down. You will probably only have four groups here based on tremendous optimism.

WIDE RECEIVERS

Everyone loves the vertical passing game. Here we will try to figure who will find the stripe and pile on the yards. You want a list of at least 40-50. We have:

1. Are they starters? Are they the #1 option or #2? (Refer to Lesson #1 team depth chart, WR1 and WR2) Looking at last years receivers there were only two #3 receivers in the league that were worthy of starting every week, Brandon Stokley of the Colts (10 TD's) and Nate Burleson of the Vikings (9 TDs).

2. What were their average TDs over the last 2 to 3 years? Did they score over 8, 9, over 10 TD's?

3. Who is their QB? Do you want Daunte Culpepper throwing to you or A. J. Feeley?

4. What does the magazine have to say? Look for insights into these questions: Any key free agent signings to take their spot? Are they still considered the starter? Is the coach making a point to get them involved more?

5. Will their team be any good? The better teams score more points in general and give their players more opportunities.

6. Are they a possession receiver or deep threat? This is a good one. Some players get 70+ catches but only 2 or 3 TD's. These guys usually lack the moves or the speed to take it to the house with a run after the catch.

8. Are they the end zone option? The new prototype receiver is the tall athletic player who runs a jumpball fade pattern for the TD. Quarterbacks do develop favorite go to guys in the red zone that they feel will help the team score, and frankly, catch the damn ball. People are paid on how many TD's they throw and catch. Drop the ball in the end zone a couple of times and you may find yourself blocking.

Last year in Pittsburgh Hines Ward had been Tommy Maddox's guy. He got hurt now all of a sudden Plaxico Burress is Big Ben's end Zone option. Culpepper had Moss, McNabb to Owens. Montana to Rice, Marino to Clayton. QB's do have favorite targets.

You will want to have at least 40 ranked.

TIGHT ENDS

Do you really have to draft one? In leagues with your friends see if you can change to 3 wide outs it can definitely add a little more scoring in your league. Tight ends benefited the most from the rules change of no contact after 5 yards as they finally were able to get down the field with out getting mugged every play. Rank 12 Tight ends because to draft two is a complete waste of a roster spot. Here we go

1. Do they use the TE frequently? The double G's were as good as most receivers in the game last year. Gates for the Chargers and Gonzalez for the Chiefs are the cream of the crop. Due to the rule changes their were a lot TE's with high catch numbers however the above two were the only ones with over 7 TD's.

2. Know the pass catching TE's from the blockers? If your tight ends nickname is old tin pockets, this is not a good thing.

3. Where does the magazine rank them and what do they say? This will give you insight on the up and comers. You want people who get the ball however if you only get points for TD's there are a few players every year who catch 20 passes and 3-4 TD's, thus making my point on waiting.

4. Good spot to look at 2nd and 3rd year players. The new wave of TE is the tall, leaper, basketball style who can just literally out jump and body any one at the goal line. The fade is

reminiscent of a lob to your center underneath in basketball.

5. Look at your sleepers and rookies here.

KICKERS

Some leagues have different scoring rules for kickers. They will have penalties for missed kicks and bonus points for distance. Double-check this before doing your rankings. Make your list 18 deep. Here we go

1. Look at the average total points over the last 2-3 years. Are they over 100 points, 110 points, 120 pts or 130 pts.? Any kicker that has been over 130 points the last couple of years is the franchise, any kicker who is below 100 points is a you have to *be kidding me*.

2. FG accuracy percentage. Be wary of any kicker that misses more than one or two inside of 40 yards, as they will be looking for new jobs by midweek. Nothing worse then finding your kicker cut. Unless you are paying attention, kickers do not get the huge headlines.

3. FG percentage over 40 yds and over 50 yds. This will usually be the bonus point FG's in some leagues. You want to make sure your kicker has tried some 50 yarders and made them with a longest hopefully at 55-53. His team will then attempt some of these kicks.

As for the over 40 yds you want a decent amount of attempts here, 9+ with only a couple misses. If your kicker cannot consistently kick his field goal from this distance, the team will be forced to go for it more on fourth down.

4. Is the kicker's offense any good to give him the opportunity to score points? Obviously, you want a team that scores many points. The Redskins and 49ers would not be good choices for kickers. Keep in mind that extra points count too. The good kickers rack up a ton of extra points.

DEFENSES

Some defenses consistently are near the top. Tampa, Philadelphia and obviously the Ravens are solid choices. However for the most part how many points a defense will score can be a bit of a guess. Leagues score defenses differently so once again know your rules because turnovers can be hard to predict however, sacks are a product of individual talents. Make your list 12 deep.

1. What do the magazines say? What do they say about last year's stats and free agent losses and upgrades? You are looking for sack totals in the 40's and high 30's, as these are 1 to 2 points in most leagues. Did they add or loose any of their big QB bell ringers.

2. Who is their coach and defensive

coordinator? Are they defensive minded coaches or new head coaches that come from a defensive system? Tradition.

3. Are their takeaways high? Fumble and especially interceptions are where you touchdowns are going to come from.

When all of your position lists are completed, you should have between 136 to 152 players ranked. Some of the smaller lists of players can go on the same page, like K and D, WR and TE. You are now in an informed position of strength heading into the draft.

Lesson #3 Draft Day Strategies

If you are new to the sport, I recommend doing Draft Day within 2 weeks of the start of the season. The closer to the start of the season draft day is the less likely of drafting a player who might still be injured or cut.

Draft Day has finally arrived, you haul ass into your friend's driveway, and you want to be the first guy at the table. Galloping in the front door your nose is filled with the aroma of Ken Davis's barbeque sauce. Your eyes quickly scan the spread and it looks like Hillshire farm little smokies in the crock pot, triscuts with paper thin cheddar cheese slices, poker chip slabs of beef summer sausage, Doritos and the proverbial big bowl of mild salsa.

We will be combining this smorgasbord with about 4 gallons of everybody's favorite carbonated beverage to drink, ok Beer. What we have here is guaranteed heartburn, BS so deep you do not dare let the pets out and an incredibly high level of testosterone.

However, by the end of the day, we will begin that magical, nerve racking, heart stopping thrill ride called a Fantasy Football season.

DRAFT DAY ORGANIZATION

First off locate a space in the draft area where you can hear everyone's picks. You want to make sure you have a comfortable location to spread out your material. If you are drafting on your computer, set up a table to put your materials on for quick reference. In some on these online drafts, you only have 90 seconds to make a pick, no time for fumbling looking for which page the depth charts are located. A little trick that can be helpful is cutting long narrow strips of paper. Cut the strips 2 to 3 inches wide and 6 inches long. Write on these slips lengthwise the names of sections you will need for quick reference.

Mark sections with your bookmarks like depth charts, QB's, RB's, NFL schedule and rookies to name a few.

Make sure you have brought everything that you used for composing your rankings. Let us start out with putting together a 12-team list of people or teams who are present. If teams names are not available just write the owners name and the number he picks at on top of the page. Make a sheet up for every owner's team like the one below. You are going to write down each owner's pick. Ideally, you have someone with you who can keep track of the players that are drafted by other teams.

DRAFT DAY ROSTER CARD

Make out your own lineup card as follows (assuming 15 rounds).

QB	1	TE	1
	2	K	1
RB	1	D	1
	2		
	3		
	4		
	5		
WR	1		
	2		
	3		
	4		
	5		

Before the draft, review your roster limits at all positions. If your league does not have a mandatory TE, you do not need to draft one. Sometimes a league will even let you draft a 6th RB however; you might run in to trouble with your bye weeks on your receivers.

After you draft a player, write him into the appropriate position spot. Then in parenthesis behind the players name, but in the number of the round you selected him. This is useful data. It will help in predicting when players will be drafted in later drafts.

As we wait for the clock to rundown on the official opening of the draft, you should now know where you are picking. Having already done your rankings based on the appropriate scoring methods, use this time to scan the mock drafts to get a feel for who will be there and start developing a game plan for your first two picks.

DRAFT DAY THEORIES

The current most popular line off thinking out there is the running back theory. The running back theory is that early in the draft, you need two or combination, at the very least; every down *franchise* or *golden boy* backs to make a run at the title. This is good advice.

However, many people follow it too literally. What I mean is the draft will start and running backs will go early and fast. Looking at the past three year trends *franchise and golden boy backs* will start running out after 8-10 players have been picked assuming they are in agreement with your rankings. Owners will then continue to pick *players of potential,* reaching for players, when based on our rankings we still have plenty of *franchise and golden boy* players at other positions.

What you are looking to do is get as many of your *franchise and golden boy* players as you can. Typically, your first round will go with 1-3 QB's, 1-

3 receivers, and 6-8 backs. (12 Teams) The run on backs will continue into the second round. By the end of the second round, 1/3 of the NFL starting running backs probably will have been picked.

It is OK to draft a QB in the first round. I know that sounds taboo, but think of Manning in the first and Harrison in the second. Alternatively, McNabb in the first and Owens in the second, an owner in our league road this all the way to 2nd place regular season finish. (Then Owens went down and McNabb didn't play, Ouch). If you do not get the receiver for the hookup, you still should get a *golden boy.* What if you drafted Reggie Wayne with the 24th pick and a good running back with the 25th? Assuming Harrison has already been drafted.

If I were to take a wide receiver in the first round like Moss, I could most certainly get Collins in the third or fourth round making for one heck of a scoring tandem.

Keep in mind that in these early rounds look at the overall cheat sheet in the magazine and on the online list. Some people will not vary much from this and it becomes quite predictable. The points to all of this being do not get locked into running back, running back, running back after the top 8 to 10 are gone. Let the draft come to you and select the best available player.

RUNS ON POSITIONS

Runs will occur through out the draft. A run is where everyone starts picking the same position pick after pick. Do not panic and are sucked in. If you are already thinking ahead, a pick or two you should know whom you want when it becomes your pick. If these two players went in the run, is the third player of the same value or do you need another position where there is higher value. I.e. *Golden boys* are still available. Typically, you will see runs early on running backs. Quarterbacks will go mid-rounds and kickers usually set off a brief run when they go.

SLEEPERS

Let us start with the definition of a sleeper. A sleeper is a player (relative unknown with low expectations) who outperforms players at his position based on where he was taken in the draft. A sleeper can be taken in any round. Typically, experienced owners do not take a sleeper until the franchise and golden boys are gone.

What makes a good sleeper is defined by the criteria we discussed in lesson #2. If the player meets the criteria and, he is a relative unknown that thru your research you have found was named the starter, he should make a good sleeper.

Typically, the second and third year player is a good candidate for a breakout year. He has learned his teams system and worked his way up the depth chart.

Rookie running backs who walk into their starting positions based on their high draft position are excellent candidates.

ROSTER POSITIONING BY ROUNDS

As you wait patiently for the person in front of you to pick in the fourth round after repeating, 2 or 3 players who have already been picked, take a quick inventory of your team. At 4 picks, I like having 2 RB's, 1 WR, and 1 QB or 2 WR, 1 RB, and 1 QB. If you do not have a quarterback by the fourth round, you will not be stuck with what is left instead of being able to choose.

Pick 5 I am looking to go running back and pick 6 is a good spot for one of your sleeper picks. Do not pick a team full of sleeper picks or you might as well name your squad the "Rip Van Winkles". Come Sunday all you will be doing is sleeping on the couch, because your boys will not be crossing the stripe, and giving you any reason to explode from the prone position.

Rounds seven and eight you might be looking at getting one of the top kickers and a good backup quarterback if still available. Others argue that kickers are a crapshoot, unpredictable, wait. This is nonsense. You can get one of the top five here and they will score 110-120 pts for you. Any kicker over 102 pts averages over 6 pts or a TD a game. Consistency scoring is what helps win the close games.

As the draft gets into the later rounds, nine thru thirteen, you will be looking at filling in your Running back and wide receiver positions. *Players with potential* here are possible goal line vultures. Guys who come in for the 1-yard plunge TD. It seems like every year there is a goal line specialist. I drafted Leonard Russell of the Denver Broncos in 1993. He had 9 TD's in helping carry me to the title.

Other players over the years who filled this role were: Bettis, M Williams, Z Crockett, M Alstott, L Hoard, B Baxter and, the Fridge.

Wide receivers that you are looking at need to be starters. Refer back to your NFL team's depth charts for any #1's left on the board. This is also a good time to explore the hookup end again. Look at the 2nd and 3rd wide outs of the QB's you have drafted. Here were some of last years late round picks that would have given you some extra punch.

M Muhammad	Carolina	16 TDs
Brandon Stokley	Indy	10 TDs
Nate Burleson	Mn	9 TDs

Marcus Robinson	MN	8 TDs
Eddie Kennison	KC	8 TDs
Ashlie Lelie	DEN	7 TDs

There also is a market for a rookie or two in this end of the draft. Last year's rookie receivers who made and impact were:

Lee Evans	Buff	9 TDs
Roy Williams	Det	8 TDs
Larry Fitzgerald	Ariz	8 TDs
Michael Clayton	TB	7 TDs

As you see rookies can make an impact at receiver and can be available late. Fitzgerald had all the press and performed quite well with rotating QB's in Arizona.

In the later rounds you also need to be checking for your bye weeks to plan accordingly. Beware of a lot of players from the same team and the same division. Do not draft two Quarterbacks that are off on the same week. Or all receivers from the AFC West and find out you have to make a couple of moves to field a complete team. If you have a good team you might not want to expose these players to waivers.

As for players on the same team I can only recommend two. No more than two players from the same team unless the third is a kicker or injury protection for a stud.

While drafting don't get obsessed with I have

to draft one of each position first to complete my team. I don't know how many drafts I've heard I have a complete team after 8 picks. You need a complete team by the end of the draft not after 8 picks. The object is to get the best players based on your personal rankings. You might end up with a 3rd and 4th running back while someone is drafting a defense or tight end to complete their team. Your 3rd or 4th running back or receiver can have a tremendous upside and help add depth. It is more important to fill in this depth, then to pick a TE, D, or even a kicker if none have been picked.

In the later rounds when there is no clear cut starter at the running back position. Some owners will draft two running backs from the same team to make sure they have that teams backfield covered. As the season progresses hopefully one of the backs they drafted will emerge as the team's starter or goal line back.

In the last two rounds pick your defense and tight end. You only need one to start the year. Defenses that are serviceable will be available all year long. In online leagues make sure you know the scoring rules for D's some have inflated point values. Defenses also are one of the first to be cut when people run into bye weeks. You can pick up a better one later.

Tight ends are a dime a dozen unless you draft Gonzalez or Gates. G & G will be gone by the third round in most drafts. That leaves all the rest. The strategy here goes that we can build depth at receiver and running back. When players start to emerge at tight end, make a move and pick them up as a free agent. Late picks at running back and wide receiver will have more value then most starting tight ends.

End of the draft picks have won me titles. I have drafted two players in the very last round of the draft that have helped me win titles. In 1996 with the last overall pick I was looking to add depth to wide receiver (we didn't have to start a tight end in that league). I looked thru my depth charts and Baltimore had a player named Michael Jackson. Vinny Testaverde was going to be their new Quarterback and Jackson was listed as a starter. Baltimore also had Brain Billick the offensive guru from the Vikes as their head coach. He met the criteria we established in the last lesson.

Jackson went on the have 18 TD's that year and took me to the finals. In the finals he did not disappoint with 3 TDs in the final game and I had another Championship.

Last year in my on line AOL fantasy football league, we have to play a mandatory TE. The scoring in this league included points for yardage. I had done the required preparation and knew who I wanted before the draft started. I was going to go with a sleeper along the lines of the new age tight ends. A player that is tall and strong with great leaping ability. I took Antonio Gates with the last pick in the draft. He scored 13 touchdowns a new tight end record. Once again, I was hoisting another trophy and thanking Mr. Gates and everyone else who made it possible.

Lesson #4 How to Use the Latest Info to Upgrade Your Team thru Free Agency and Trades

When the draft is over do not throw away all your accumulated info. Get a 3-ring binder and put in everyone's team in order. Also place your ranking sheets in the binder. Be organized in everything you do for the year. Use your weekly binder to write down your transactions and weekly lineups, including your opponents. Date the top of the page to correspond to the game dates.

Now that we have everything in the binder review everyone's teams. Check your personal rankings and make sure everyone who was drafted is crossed off. Double check now to make sure you didn't cross off anyone that wasn't drafted. Now, between your magazines and your personal ranking you have a list of free agents that you will start to key on.

If everything is computerized you still want to print out every ones team roster. Print the total draft and the free agent spreadsheet and get it in a binder. You will be able to browse over this binder at odd times when the computer is unavailable.

(Like when you have to get up at 2 am to get any PC time on the weekends, because the kids are tying up the computer playing games or surfing the net.)

Now go over every team and look at their depth. Get to know everyone's teams because you want to be in tune with all the other teams in the league and their needs. This will help you not lose players in waivers to other teams. Specifically if I know Bubbas Brickhousers are going to have two of their starting running backs on bye in week 8, and I've been looking at picking up an up and comer back, I will make my move in week 7. Also knowing everyone's team will give us ideas for starting the trade mill.

The season has started and the first games have been played. It's Monday morning and you're ready to do the official scoring. I highly recommend getting an online stat capable service like Fanball.com. If you play in an online league your scoring will be live which is nice. Whether you are online or not, you want to get the Monday morning paper. USA today works well or the local paper if they cover the NFL with box scores.

READING A BOX SCORE

What you want in your news paper is a complete box score. Going thru this will tell you who is getting the ball.

Here is a recreated fictional box score:

Vikings 30 Lions 27

Seattle	3	7	7	10	-	27
St Louis	3	10	7	10	-	30

First Quarter
Minn: FG Andersen 35 Yds, 12:52
Detroit: FG Hanson 45 Yds, 5:22
Tied 3-3

Second Quarter
Detroit: Pinner 5 yd run (Hanson kick), 14:22
Minn: Burleson 15 yd pass from Culpepper (Andersen), 7:02
Minn: FG Andersen 52 Yds, :03
Minnesota 13-10

Third Quarter
Minn: Campbell 35 yd pass from Culpepper (Andersen kick), 12:25
Detroit: Williams 12 yd pass from Harrington (Hanson kick) 3:25
Minnesota 20-17

Fourth Quarter
Detroit: K Jones 35 yd run (Hanson kick), 10:01
Detroit: FG Hanson 25 yds, 7:22

Minn: B Williams 45 yd Interception return (Andersen kick), 4:50
Minn: FG Andersen 22 yds, :35
Minnesota 30-27

Team Statistics

	Det	Minn
First Downs	20	22
Rushing	10	8
Passing	10	14
Penalty	0	0
3rd down eff	3-12	5-11
4th down eff	1-1	0-0
Total Net yds	375	470
Total plays	62	68
Avg Gain	5.2	7.1
Net Yds rushing	225	165
Rushes	30	25
Avg Yds per rush	7.5	6.6
Net Yds passing	150	305
Completed Attempted	14-31	27-40
Yards per pass	4.8	7.6
Sacked-yds lost	1-5	3-17
Had intercepted	1	0
Punts-average	3-48.3	3-45.8
Return Yardage	22	11
Punts-returns	2-22	1-11
Kickoffs-returns	6-170	7-156

Interceptions-returns	0-0	1-45
Penalties-yards	3-20	5-30
Fumbles-lost	1-0	1-2
Time of possession	26:45	33:15

Player Statistics
Missed field goals: Minnesota (Andersen 49 wr)

Detroit rushing: K Jones 25-195, Pinner 1-5
S Bryson 4-25

Minnesota rushing: M Bennett 18-150, O Smith 5-10, Culpepper 2-5

Detroit passing: Harrington 10-25 for 100 yds, 1 Int, 1 TD. M McMahon 4-6 for 50 yds.

Minnesota passing: Culpepper 26-39 for 250, 0 Int, 2 TD's, Mo Williams 1-1 for 55 yds

Detroit receiving: Williams 5-75, Swinton 5-35, C Rogers 4-30, K Jones 1-10

Minnesota receiving: Burleson 7-130 (1TD), Williamson 8-90, K Campbell 6-50 (1 TD), Mo Williams 5-30, M Bennett 1-5

Detroit Tackle-assists-sacks Bryant 6-0-0, Walker 6-0-0, Wilkinson 3-1-3

Minnesota Tackle-assists-sacks Winfield 7-2-0, D Thomas 5-0-0, B Williams 5-0-0

Turnovers-Interceptions: Minnesota (B Williams 1 for 45 yds, TD) fumbles lost: Minnesota (Culpepper)

Now as you sit down Monday Night to watch the last match up for the week grab the box score page and a yellow highlighter. What we are going to do is go thru and highlight all the free agents.

Being that you have reviewed everyone's team plus you have it available in your binder, this should be a simple process. Looking at the above box score:

Detroit: Pinner 5 yard run

Minn: Burleson 12 yard pass from Culpepper

Culpepper was obviously drafted but somebody might not have taken Burleson yet. (The guy is going to be a stud). And who the heck is Pinner?

You now should be asking yourself is Pinner the goal line guy in Detroit. Did K Jones get hurt or did he come out for a blow after a long run? Pinner is a free agent, highlight him.

Next I am highlighting K Campbell. Any receiver on Minnesota deserves consideration with a QB like Culpepper. R Williams should have been drafted somewhere in the middle rounds but double check. Harrington might be out there for a backup QB.

Ok now we go to the player statistics (Above). This will tell you about performance in yardage leagues and who is getting the ball.

Detroit rushing: There is Pinner and his 1-5 (one carry for 5 yards) and a TD. He could be a goal line guy. Bryson 4-25. Detroit was using 3 backs. Highlight Bryson.

Minnesota rushing: Looks like Bennett was the man this game. Michael Bennett should have been drafted as well as Onterio Smith.

Looking at the passing line: Culpepper is drafted. Interesting line under Detroit. Did they get sick of Harrington and give him the hook? Did he get hurt? If you have Joey on your bench this situation is alarming and requires watching for info. We will talk later about places to look for updates.

Receiving: Detroit who is this Swinton guy? Highlight Swinton. It looks like C Rogers is back from injury. Highlight C Rogers. For Minnesota we already checked on Burleson and Campbell. Who is this Williamson? The rookie from South Carolina is getting some PT (playing time) baby.

Any rookie that is getting the ball a lot and performing could be a serious sleeper. He is also at a position that put out some nice performers as rookies last year. Highlight Williamson.

Continue this thru all the box scores for the week. It will take a little while at first but as you get familiar with the players, and the players that were drafted in will go faster. When you are done keep the box score part of the paper for referral on transaction day.

If you play in online leagues this is still an important exercise to help you see who is getting the ball consistently. Online leagues will usually list the free agents with the top players in scoring by your league rules going down. It will give you who has scored the most but it won't give you the feel for how involved in the offense. Did the guy at the top of the list score all his points in two games? Did he lose his job and is now a third wide out?

If you looked at the above box score would you pick up K Campbell because he scored or Williamson because of his tremendous upside? The point in all this is that by reading box scores you know who is involved in the offense and getting the ball. Last I checked there are no points for playing catch on the sideline.

HOW TO USE WEEKLY LEADER BOARDS

Another good exercise can be accomplished when the local paper comes out with the NFL statistical leaders. In the USA today it is on Wednesdays. Open the paper up get out the highlighter and highlight everyone who was not drafted.

The first place you want to start is the most obvious. Touchdown or scoring lists depending on the publication you are looking at. You would be surprised how long some players will be on this leader board before someone will pick them up. This is especially true early in the year when everyone still has confidence in the Travis Henry's and Lee Suggs's of the year.

Passers: In USA today they are ranked by passer rating. This might affect you if you have penalty points for interceptions; otherwise we are only interested about tossing the rock IN THE ZONE.

Furthermore, this is a good place to pickup that second kicker. Once the season has started, you're going to need another one for the bye. Kicker's is an easy place to pickup consistent points. Just look thru the leader board highlight your guys and watch their stats and upcoming match ups.

Defenses can be upgrade here. USA today breaks down the defense by yardage. In most fantasy leagues defensive scoring is based on TD's, sacks, and takeaways. The USA doesn't give you TD's, but gives turnovers information in table format.

The sack totals are also listed and can be found under the team defense tables. Look under passing heading and sacks have their own column. The first number is the number of sacks; the second number in parenthesis is their league rank.

You can also find the interception totals for a team. It is the next column over from the sack column. Same format.

INJURY REPORT

So now we are just about ready for transaction date. We have one last place to check before we are armed and ready to make our weekly pickups. The injury report. It comes out on Thursdays. Here is how to read it.

Probable	75% will play
Questionable	50%
Doubtful	25%
Out	0 %

This can be very useful report to make sure your players are on the field game time. If your guy is questionable or lower on the injury report, and you have no other options on your team, make a move in free agency to complete your lineup. Now that you have done your homework, let's make a move.

TRANSACTION REPORT

Depending on when your draft was, you need to watch the waiver wire to see if any of your players get cut in a salary cap move, injured, or beat out by a rookie. You need to be especially aware of kickers. In the USA today and in most local papers the waiver report is in the scoreboard page. Look under transactions for the latest waiver moves made by the NFL teams. This is a great place to tell you who's been cut and signed.

Other than a serious injury, you should wait to make a move until at least a game or two has been played. I call it my Marcus Allen rule. 1993, I picked Marcus Allen in the last round when he had just gone to KC. He met all the criteria, starter, number one guy and a good offense. I cut him after the first week and he went on to score 15 TDs' that year. The guy who picked him up went to the championship.

Even if your team is going to remain idle for a week or two, make sure to watch other team's waivers. It is important to keep every team rosters updated in your binder. People have a tendency to forget about players because they were drafted. You need to check to see if they get cut.

By week 2 of checking box scores and watching our team we should start to get a feel for the red zone players. You also will start to get an idea of were you are as a team, your weaknesses your strengths, and your depth.

Week 3 also will be the first of the bye weeks so plan accordingly.

Remember you are looking for depth in the backfield. It is also a good time to start looking for another kicker. You want 2 kickers on your roster unless you have a kicker on a team that is scoring 30-40 pts a game.

By the middle weeks of the season you will know who the NFL offensive juggernauts are as they continue to put up the points. Get a piece of the action while the getting is good. Too many people wait to long to make a move. Last year players like Michael Bennett, Travis Henry, Marshall Faulk, and Santana Moss come to mind as being held on to too long. Trade them while they still have promise and intrigue with other owners.

TRADES

Now is the time to begin looking at trades to improve your team. Ideally you have some depth at a position, preferably running back. People are always looking to trade for a running back as they get into trouble with injuries or bye weeks. Trade a running back to upgrade a receiver or quarterback. A high flying running back that comes on with a couple of TD games in a row can be a hot commodity. There was nobody hotter last year after Quentin Griffins Monday night performance against KC. He looked like he had won the position permanently and you could have cashed in for a proven commodity from a team feeling desperate after week one.

When exploring a trade remember what you are trying to accomplish. You want to add a quality starter at another position you feel you are weak. The ideal player has good match ups in weeks 14-17, depending on when your playoffs take place. On any free agent pickup you should always be building a team to win the championship.
In other words you want players who will have the most favorable match ups in the playoffs. This may help you decide between two fairly even free agents.

PROTECTION STRATEGY
You should always be on the look out to upgrade your team. As the bye weeks come thru, and you start commit to starting a running back or two every

week, and possibly a quarterback on a top team, you want to start looking to protect your studs.
It is time to invest in some injury protection policies. Many teams with solid backups would have solid starters if the player in front of them on the depth chart gets hurt. Backups on the same team as your studs deserve immediate consideration. You don't want to have your fellow owners watching the injury report and snatching these players up from under your nose.

For example, when you have gotten thru your bye weeks and have committed to starting the Chief's or the Jets running back every week. You want to take out insurance policies by the name of Larry Johnson (KC) or D Blaylock coverage in NY for the rest of the year. Backup running backs last year that saw serious playtime and produced were:

J Bettis	13 TD's and 941 yds
L Johnson KC	9 TD's and 581 yds
D Blaylock KC	9 TD's and 539 yds
R Droughns Den	6 TD's and 1240 yds
N Goings Car	6 TD's and 821 yds

You even got some contributions from C Taylor in Baltimore, and Chatman in San Diego.

The lesson here is if you are committed to using that teams back every week, it is smart to pickup the backup to protect your initial investment. This strategy can be very effective after your teams have gone thru the byes. A team's season can go down the toilet with one ACL and no depth.

Lesson #5 Who Do I Start?

Now that we have our roster defined we are ready to ponder the never ending perplexing question of …. Who the heck should I start this week?

INJURY REPORT

This is the first place you should start every week. On every Thursday in the newspapers, web sites or other publications comes the NFL injury report. Teams are required to submit an injury report. Players that are listed as probable, you always play. Questionable, depends on my other options at the position. Most of the time if a guy is questionable I will sit him until I can get an update on his condition on game day. Players listed as doubtful and out, never play them unless they are upgraded.

On game day, Fox, ESPN, and CBS will have update on the status of injured players. They typically have a ticker line going on the screen that will give you weather and injury updates. Some players will be upgrade, which mean their probability of playing has increased, or downgraded, the opposite. Always look at the injury report before you finalize your lineup.

STARTING LINEUPS

Assuming you had no injuries that forced you to make any unexpected moves. How about the first week you start.... The top picks you made at each of the required positions.

Your number 1 QB
1 and 2 RB's
Your top 2 wide outs, the third one can be best match up.
Only TE
Only D
Only K at this point.

Unless you have a "can't lose" match up. You drafted these players based on all your painstaking research, give them a shot.

After the first week we start getting a little more scientific as we start to get more information on your player performance and the competitions that he will face.

STUDS

You will want to start your *franchise players* every week. Ideally, you should have a #1 running back and a #1 receiver you pencil in to the lineup every week no matter what. The only exception is if they obviously lose their job to lack of production or injury.

Unless you have one of the top 4 or 5 QB's,

quarterback is a position you can rotate fairly effectively. Thus the importance of drafting 2 good quarterbacks or acquiring a second one off the waiver wire later. You will see how this played out in lesson 7 a Championship run. We'll discuss kicker, TE and D later.

ANALYZING FOR FAVORABLE MATCH UPS

Week 1 is in the books and hopefully you have the big W. You've read your box scores to study the waiver wire, and after the first game you have some players who are getting the ball and you like them as starters.

Now we want to look at the paper when the league stats come out. Obviously the first week the info is limited but as the season goes on this will be a valuable tool. You will be looking at individual player match ups, against the defenses they are playing that week.

In USA today the statistics are printed on Wednesdays in the sports section. What you are looking at are the individual team defenses. They have a ranking that will show how many yards against the pass a team gives up. How many yards against the run is the team giving up. How many points have they given up as a team?

For instance, you're probably looking at one or two different receivers to start? Receiver K

Johnson is going against a team giving up 260 yds a game passing and the J Smith is up against a team giving up 170 yards a game. All other things being equal start K Johnson. These are the match up edges you are looking to capitalize on.

COUNTER PLAY MATCH UP STRATEGY

To continue on the wide receiver angle, you can make a counter play to your opponent's lineup.

Basketball coaches are known for doing a lot of counter lineups. If you play John scorer, I will counter with Joe rebounder. If you go big, I'll counter your lineup with going smaller and faster. In Fantasy football you can use this strategy at the receiver and quarterback position.

The match up play goes like this. I know who my opponent is playing at quarterback, and one of my receivers plays for the same team. I start that receiver to help offset the points he gets from his quarterback. This can be especially effective when having to choose from limited or less then ideal match ups due to byes or injuries.

Say for example he has Culpepper (who had a couple of 5 TD games last year), and you have M Robinson or even J Wiggins in a mandatory Tight End league. Culpepper throws 3 against you but one was to Robinson or Wiggins. Now you only need two from your QB. You get the idea.

Defenses are great candidates for counter play match up. You can effectively rotate this position weekly thru free agency looking for favorable match ups. Start the defenses that are at home against inferior opponents.

THE LINE STRATEGY

When you are still stuck and can't seem to find a clear edge on which kicker to start, you can get a little help from the odds makers. Go to the scoreboard section of your paper and look at the over/under number for the games your kicker is playing in. The line in the paper will tell you who is favored and give you the total points for betting over that number or under. If one is 47 (total points scored by both clubs) and one is 33, with everything else being equal that makes it pretty easy to decide who I will start.

You can also use this angle for picking up a free agent or two for a game because of a bye or injury. Basically if you wanted to pickup a player for a cup of coffee (a one game spot start) and couldn't decide from two equal match ups. Go with the game the pros think are going to produce more points, the higher over/under number.

OTHER CONSIDERATIONS

Another ingredient in trying to decide who to start

is, let's say you have 2 RB's performing about the same fighting for the second starting position on the roster. Start the home player. Teams score more points at home than on the road. When in doubt and you don't know who to start with all things being equal. Start the hometown player.

As we get later in the year we have some box scores at our fingertips to help us with the divisional match ups. Every team plays each team in its division 2 times. After the first match up between the teams is in the books, when it becomes time to play that team again, dig out your free agent box scores and see who performed and who didn't.

Check out our recreated box score in the previous lesson between Detroit and Minnesota who play twice a year. There was a lot of offense (points and yards) in this game and K Jones and M Bennett make solid plays. You could make an argument for both kickers and the Minnesota passing offense also.

Weather can be another determining factor in who to start. This is why we love those dome players. Fox, ESPN, and CBS all have weather girls or reports on Sunday. Games later in the year in the northern latitudes present some problems for the passing game unless you're Brett Farve. In Denver it might be snowing. New York is always windy making it tough to kick and throw. You get the idea.

Never mess with a player on a streak. If a player gets hot and is scoring every week, leave him in there. Don't over manage. Let him post a goose egg before you even think about taking him out of the lineup. And even then if he is still getting the ball a lot, which we can see by watching our box score's, I probably wouldn't pull him either.

The kicking position can provide you a touchdown a game (6 pts). You should be able to play the rotating kicker game. The best place to start is where my kicker ranks on the leader board. If he isn't in the top six in either the AFC or NFC by his teams fifth game played you definitely need to do some upgrading.

After you have two kickers on your roster. Here are some things to consider: Which team consistently scores more points. The league standings in the paper give you the points for and the points against for each team. Which kicker is playing the team with the worst defense? Which kicker is at home? Is one kicking indoors which leads to longer field goal chances and coaches taking more cracks at it?

If you are able to access the web there is also a plethora of web sites that will break down the weekly match ups. Type in Fantasy Football and you will get close to 500 web sites. Some of these web sites will give you weekly breakdowns of match ups and recommend starters. Fanball.com does a good job of breaking down the individual player match ups. There is a listing of fantasy football websites in appendix III.

Lastly, call in your lineup. It is advantageous to enter your lineup early online or get it called in to your commissioner. Get those bye week changes out of the way right away. You can always make changes later. (Check to see how many lineup changes are allowed)

Typically what I've seen having been a former commissioner also, is life happens. People get busy with their day to day life and the next thing they know its Sunday 11:55 am and they are scrambling to figure everything out. Calling in a lineup early to at least figure out your bye weeks has saved many a team. You can fine tune the individual match ups later but at least if something were to happen you have a complete team.

To summarize:

1. Have your Monday box scores
2. Have you Tuesday box score (Monday Night Game)
3. Have your Wednesday USA league Statistics
4. Thursday the injury report comes out. Read the injury report over completely

5. Make your free agent transactions.
6. Call in your lineup 1st edition replacing injured or bye week players
7. Check your websites for updated injury info and individual match up analysis.
8. Use the tips and data we have gathered above to complete a lineup.
9. Call in your revised lineup.

Lesson #6 How to Play Fantasy Football. Including Different Methods and Optional Rules

Having read the book to this point, I am thinking your face has been painted with your favorite teams colors. Two tone, one check purple the other gold. You're purple 84 Moss jersey has been replaced with your Daunte, number 11. You are beginning to gather predraft information and are crossing off days on your calendar in anticipation of the Sweet Sounds of September.

Hopefully you can gather enough colleagues together to do a draft party and start your own league. Draft day is a rite of passage for every football enthusiast, from causal observer or participant to the hard core. It gets in your blood and is intoxicating as a new romance.

What I am going to do is give you some basic options you can choose from to put together your own fantasy football league. Some of these options that I have listed are based on all my years experience as a commissioner and an owner playing this fun and exciting game.

If you do not have enough people or the time

to create your own league, you can always play online. Is owning a computer a problem? Your library offers online use of the computer. Typically if you do your research ahead of time based on our system above, you could go to the library on Thursday or later and submit a well thought out lineup. I have seen publications including newspapers that offer leagues. Typically they have choices of groups of players, and you select x amount of groups to form a team. This would be another way to get involved.

Ok let's get started. You have found 8, 10, or 12 football nuts like yourself who want to get a league going. Start by selecting a commissioner. The commissioner is responsible for setting up the rules, draft, and keeping track of all transactions. He also checks the scoring and weekly results as well as publishes the standings. I would recommend having a stat service or an assistant commissioner to help with the scoring, administrative duties as well as a backup for coverage.

There are many different rules for fantasy football and I will lay out some options that you can use in any form or manner to create your very own league of Sunday excitement. By choosing different combinations of these rules you will develop your own feel for what you want for your league and where you are going in the future.

THE DRAFT

There are two styles of drafts that are commonly used. The auction style uses a salary cap of a random number. For argument purposes we will say $250. Each owner has $250 total to field a roster of a predetermined amount of players. 15 to 16 man rosters are fairly standard.

At the start of the draft the commissioner will pick a name, say Peyton Manning and start the bidding. The minimum bid for each player is $1. Owners will bid on how much of their $250 total salary cap for their team they will tie up in Peyton Manning. After Peyton is signed say for $50 (highest bidder), that owner has $200 left to spend for the rest of his team.

This process continues with each owner nominating a player for bid, which if he nominates he must bid on, until everyone has a full team. Each owner must have at least one dollar for each open position on his team. As owners fill their rosters, they drop out of the bidding process.

The other type of draft process is the serpentine style, straight pick'em draft. Typically you take a set of cards. Remove the top 12 spades (assuming 12 teams) put them on a table and have each individual draw a card. The ace of spades is the number one pick in the draft.

The owner of the number one pick makes his selection and that player is his to put on his roster. This process continues thru the 12th pick, where that owner starts the second round with the 13th pick. The second round ends with the owner who started the draft picking the 24th player and he starts the 3rd round (25th pick) and so on.

Based on a 15-16 round draft you need to set some roster limits on positions:

3 QB's
5 RB's
6 WR's
2 TE's
2 K's
2 D's

This does not mean you have 20 people on the roster, but that a team may only have at a maximum these limits at any of the six scoring positions. You may have any combination of these limits as set by your league rules to get to your 15 or 16 players limit. If you go any more than this at any position, the free agent pool becomes too thin.

Types of starting Lineups: Each starting lineup contains 8 players total. Of those 8 players there are 5 to 6 positions that make up your lineup. There are various options for choosing your required

starting lineups.
Here are 3:

1. 1 QB, 2 RB's, 2 WR's, 1 TE, 1 K, 1 D

2. 1 QB, 2 RB's, 3 WR's, 1 K, 1 D
   or 1 QB, 2 RB's, 1 WR, 2 TE's, 1 K, 1 D
   or 1 QB, 2 RB's, 2 WR's, 1 TE, 1 K, 1 D

3. 1 QB, 2 RB, 2 WR, 1 TE, 1 K, 1 D
   Or 1 QB, 1 RB, 3 WR, 1 TE, 1 K, 1 D.

I personally prefer option #2, as it gives you much more flexibility at the receivers, tight end position.

SCORING
We have many different avenues to explore here.
Basic: Scoring in this league is based on touchdowns.

All players 6 points for a touchdown rushing
2 points for a 2 point conversion rushing
6 points for a touchdown receiving
2 points for a 2 point conversion receiving
6 or 4 points for a touchdown passing.
2 points for a 2 point conversion passing. (You must pick between awarding 6 points for a passing

touchdown or 4 points.) 6 points puts a huge emphasis on quarterback which is fine.

Kickers 3 points for a FG
1 point for a PAT

Defense 6 points for a defensive touchdown, returned punt, or kick return, 2 points for a safety

Performance: Scoring in this league is based on yardage gain by a player.

1 point for every 10 yards rushing
1 point for every 10 yards receiving
1 point for every 20 yards passing

Kickers 3 points for a FG from 0-39 yds
4 points for a FG from 40-49 yds
5 points for a FG from 50+
1 point for a PAT

Defense 1 point for a sack, 1 point for an interception, 1 for a fumble lost, 2 points for a safety, there is also scoring based on amount of yardage given up or points given up.

Combination: This combines the two scoring leagues 6 points for touchdowns, and extra performance points for yardage as described in the performance league. Kickers and defense you can choose either method. Combination leagues that use both scoring methods above result in high scoring games. If you don't, play online or subscribe to a stat service, this can be a little time consuming scoring games. It is extremely exciting as you are always "in the game."

Some leagues like to use a variation of the basic and performance points. Here is another option, the scoring that was used in one of last year's championship runs. Combo variation:

All players	6 points for all touchdowns as described above in the basic and bonus points for performance 3 points for every 100 yards rushing 2 points for every 50 yards after the initial 100 yards rushing 3 points for every 100 yards receiving 2 points for every 50 yards after the initial 100 yards receiving 3 points for every 300 yards passing. 1 point for every 50 yards passing After the initial 300 yards passing
Kickers	3 points for a field goal 1 point for a PAT
Defense	6 points for defensive touchdown, 6 points for a kickoff or punt return, 1 point for a sack, 1 point

for an interception, 2 points for a safety.

Optional Rules

Over the years there have been many interesting rules. Here are a few, you might like some or bust out laughing on others.

Rotisserie Style: The first one is actually a different type of format for playing Fantasy Football. It is Fantasy Football with a Rotisserie Style standing system.

Everybody turns in a lineup just like regular leagues; however there are no individual match ups. Everybody plays everybody. When the games are over, all scores are added up and ranked. Each team receives a point total based on where they ranked compared to everyone else that week.

Ex. 10 Team league

Blue fish scored 48 fantasy pts	10 pts
Red Bird scored 47 fantasy pts	9 pts
Yellow Dog scored 45 fantasy pts	8 pts
Green Walrus scored 39 fantasy pts	7 pts
Black Eel scored 30 fantasy pts	6 pts

These points are then added each week for a cumulative total. If there is a tie, you get .5 points. If 3 teams tie then you add up the number of points for the rankings and divide by number of teams.

9+8+7/3 = 8

Ex:		
	Red Bird scored 22 fantasy pts	10 pts
	Yellow Dog scored 20 fantasy pts	8
	Black eel scored 20 fantasy pts	8
	Green Walrus scored 20 fantasy pts	8
	Blue Fish scored 19 fantasy pts	6

So after 2 weeks the cumulative standings would be

Red Bird	19 pts
Yellow Dog	16 pts
Blue Fish	16 pts
Green Walrus	15 pts
Black Eel	14 pts

This league will run all 17 weeks as there are no playoffs. Winner is at the top of the standings at the end.

No OT games: Every team calls in a reserve lineup ranking their bench players. The home team gets first crack at winning the game. You take their 1st player on the list of nonstarters and if that player scored a touchdown or kicked a field goal that team wins. If there is no score with the first player, the visiting team goes to his first player. You go back and forth until you get a winner. It's kind of like a shootout in soccer.

A slight variation of this is each team chooses one player for overtime. Which ever player scores more fantasy points wins. This is more effective in performance leagues as the points will vary more.

Keeper leagues: These tend to be longstanding groups of owners who have the initial draft and keep their players for a set amount of time. Players who are cut are eligible for the free agent pool in next year's draft. You have a set amount of players that are protected from year to year. Not as common a league.

Keeper player: You get to keep the 5th round pick of you draft for three years. This was interesting and added a lot of rookies and kickers going in the 5th round. After 3 years the player is returned to the pool. Fun rule if you have the majority of owners returning every year.

One running back rule: The weekly lineup only needs to start one running back (if they want). The owner starts four players at any combination at the wide receiver and tight end positions, and only one running back.

Ex.	1 QB	1 K
	1 RB	1 D
	1 WR	
	1 WR	
	1 WR	
	1 TE	

This will change the strategy of the draft for some owners. Another benefit is it gives more flexibility with bye weeks, injuries, and lack of running back depth.

Defensive player: This one is quite popular. During the draft everyone drafts 1 defensive player and gets points for tackles, sacks, interceptions and any individual touchdowns. Individual tackles are listed in box score we created. Check Minnesota: Winfield 7-2-0. He would get 7 points. Obviously defensive players under this system will score big points.

Scoring options: Points for completions, receptions, attempts. Some leagues give a point for 10 receptions, 10 rushing attempts is one point, and 10 completions is one point. You can pick the number to set it at. Other notable ones, -2 for interceptions throw by a QB, -1 for player fumbles, 10 points for a defensive shutout

Team QB and K: When drafting, an owner drafts a team and he gets its starting quarterback. He gets both quarterbacks statistics for that team in any game. Same concept with the kicker. Basically if your quarterback gets hurt and his backup comes in and throws three TD's you get the points for it. I like the team kicker better than quarterback.

Pick a coach. Pick a coach for the week and if their team wins you get 3 points. ??? Yeah that's what I thought.

When choosing a scoring system I would suggest a combination scoring platform. This will add more excitement to a basic league where scores tend to be low.

Let's refer to our previous box score for some examples. We will us the Quarter 1 thru 4 for **basic** scoring purposes and score each player

Running backs	Pinner	6 pts
	K Jones	6 pts
Receivers	Burleson	6 pts
	Campbell	6 pts
	R Williams	6 pts
Passing	Culpepper	12 pts (6 per pass)
		8 pts (4 per pass)
	Harrington	6 pts (6 per pass)
		4 pts (4 per pass)
Kicking	Andersen	12 pts
	Hanson	9 pts
Defense	Minnesota	6 pts
	Detroit	0 pts

87 points scored.

For **Performance** Scoring we get:

Rushing	Bennett	15 pts
	O Smith	1 pt
	K Jones	19 pts
	Bryson	2 pts
Receiving	Burleson	13 pts
	Williamson	9 pts
	Campbell	5 pts
	Mo Williams	3 pts
	R Williams	7 pts
	Swinton	3 pts
	Rogers	3 pts
	Jones	1 pt
Passing	Culpepper	12 pts
	Harrington	5 pts
Kicking	Andersen	14 pts
	Hanson	10 pts
Defense	Minnesota	8 pts
	Detroit	4 pts

134 points scored.

Select a system that you will use for the year and in

future years don't be afraid to add, subtract or adjust your scoring for maximum satisfaction. The idea is to have fun. One way that really improves any football match up on TV is having a guy going who you can cheer for. In my opinion some type of combination scoring adds to the enjoyment of watching these games. With a combination league even low scoring games can produce points for your league and team.

Season Logistics: Now that we know our method of draft and scoring, we need to set up our divisions and schedule. Some leagues use the draft order as the team numbers also. Other leagues draw cards for team number first and then for draft order.

Once you have your total number of teams you can run your league a few different ways.

Option A: 8 teams, 2 divisions. Top 4 teams make the playoffs. Division A winner and Division B winner then the next 2 best teams record wise. Seed 1 vs. 4, 2 vs. 3 or top 6 teams make playoffs teams 1 and 2 (division winners) get byes the first week of the playoffs. 3 plays 6, 4 plays 5. Reseed after round. Lowest remaining seed plays number 1 seed.

Option B: 10 teams, 2 divisions. Playoff same as format above with 4 or 6 teams making the playoffs.

Option C: 12 teams, 3 divisions. 6 teams make the playoffs. All division winners are in, with the top 2 getting a first round bye. 3 plays 6, 4 plays 5. Reseed.

For an 8, 10, and 12 team schedule see Appendix IV.

Some leagues also have a play down or consolation bracket. Traditionally called the Toilet Bowl. You take the worst 4 or 6 teams and bracket them in playoff format with the loser moving on. In other words you need to win to get out of the bowl. The loser of that tournament (the team that loses all the way thru) brings the beer, pop, or food to next years draft party.

TRANSACTIONS

Now we have our schedule. The next piece of business is deciding how to handle transactions. Transactions include everything from free agents, to trades, to writing down starting lineups.

It is highly recommended to get a stat service like Fanball.com. This will do everything online and has many different ways to handle the weekly functions.

Even if you do set up an online service sometimes not everyone in your league will have access to a computer. You will still have to handle some general managing over the phone.

Start by deciding which day of the week transactions can be executed. Thursday is a great day to start because the injury report comes out and this report will generate many of a teams moves as discussed in chapter 4. When there is a Thursday game, switch transactions to Wednesday.

Tell every owner the first day of transactions is Thursday with the above exception and you must call in by 10:00 pm. Players are then awarded by which ever method you decide promotes equality and fair play. Here are some different criteria you can use for awarding free agents: player goes to the team with the worst record, or least total points scored overall, or least total points scored that week.

However you decide to award the player, think about going with one player only on the first day. This keeps owners from completely overhauling their teams before anyone has a chance to pick any one up.

After Thursday night deadline, transactions are open until 10 minutes before the first game on Sunday. You might want to put a limit on the number of moves a team can make if your league is not online. Let teams make one, two, or three moves a week. This will force teams to plan ahead and watch their bye weeks instead of driving you and other league owners crazy at deadline time.

All players cut from a team are frozen until the following week so everyone has a chance to pickup a Marcus Allen. See earlier report.

STARTING LINEUPS

Now that everyone has brought their free agents in and tendered those contracts, it is time to set the weekly lineup.

There are multiple options for approaching starting lineups. Here are a few:

1. All lineups are due by 10 minutes before the first game of the week. Keep in mind there are weeks with Thursday games and Saturday games. This will lock a player in on Thursday for Sunday whether he gets hurt or not.

2. All players who are involved in a particular game must be called in 10 minutes before that game. Example: Rufus's Redzone Raiders has 2 guys playing Thursday he calls them in.
He has 3 guys going in Sunday's noon game, which he calls in at 11:30. 1 in Sunday evening game he calls after the first game, and 2 on Monday night. This option is an administrative nightmare unless it is set up online.

3. The final option is any players that play early on Thursday and Saturday must be called in 10 minutes prior to the first game of that day. Sunday and Monday players are called in 10

minutes before Sunday's first game. This is my favorite option.

If you are not online, it is a must to have voice mail or answering machine with a time stamp.

League Standings

We now need a way to establish the overall standings. Once again the options are varied:

1. Won-Loss-Ties record with total fantasy points as a tie breaker.
2. Won-Loss-Ties record with divisional record as first tie breaker, and total fantasy points as the next tie breaker

In the second format, your standings will include an overall standings and divisional record standings. The last column will be total fantasy points like so:

Overall			Division			
Wins	Loses	Ties	Wins	Loses	Ties	Total Points
4	2	0	3	1	0	320
4	2	0	2	2	0	331
3	3	0	2	2	0	290
2	4	0	1	3	0	265

The teams are in order by first, second, third, and fourth. Notice that team two has more total points and in option one format would be in first place. However in this format, games in the division are huge. The last games of the schedule against division opponents will make or break your season. The intensity of these rivalries will boil your blood like Packers vs. Vikes, Cowboys vs. Redskins, Pittsburg vs. Cleveland and Da Raiders vs. Da Broncos.

PLAYOFFS

You have to decide now on how long the season will last and when the playoffs will begin. This will bring up one of the never ending debates, is the championship week played in week 16 or week 17. You can make debates for each cause. Week 16 Championships have the advantages of starters less likely to be rested because there is still playoff seeding to be decided in the NFL.

Last year this was a factor in week 16 with McNabb seeing limited action and Westbrook not playing at all, because of the Eagles wrapping up the number one playoff seed.

Week 17 was the same with McNabb, and some other studs not playing full games like Peyton Manning and Drew Brees.

The other side of the argument is you take a week out of the season, losing entertainment value and weekly visual stimuli.

To build a championship team you must have depth. If you have planned ahead, looked at your scheduled match ups, and have solid backup players, you should be able to win a title based on everything you‘ve learned regardless of which week is the title game.

Now use one of the formats from season logistics. Work backwards from your championship week of 16 or 17 and this will give you your season length.

You have everything you need to enjoy the passion of fantasy football. Take notes, and keep your binder and notebook updated. This will help you with modifications to your league in future years. Everything needs an adjustment as the years turn into decades, don’t get stale and try new things.

Lesson #7 A Case Study. 2004 Championship Season

The purpose of this chapter is to take you thru the thought process of a championship season. We will use the lessons taught to us above and apply them to what happen during the season. We will also critique the errors that proved costly during the season. You learn from your mistakes.

I won 2 fantasy football championships last year. One was online AOL league and the other was a traditional league with my friends that many off us have been involved in for over ten memory filled years. I will touch briefly on some of the important points (learning tools) of the AOL league and then begin an in-depth look at our traditional league week by week.

The AOL league was a performance/scoring combination league. 6 points for a rushing and receiving touchdown, 4 points for a passing TD with 2 points bonus points for longer touchdowns. 1 point for every 10 yards rushing or receiving. 1 point for every 20 yards passing. Field Goals were distance based and defenses got 2 points per sack, 2 points per int, 1 point per fumble. Inflated scoring.

Starting lineups consisted of a mandatory TE however you could play 3 wide outs, 1 tight end and 1 running back if you wanted to.

The draft was one of the earlier ones. August 15th and I had the 8th pick.

Here is the team I drafted and the round in parenthesis where I got some of my key players.

QB	1. D Culpepper (1)
	2. D Carr
RB	1. T Barber (4)
	2. C Brown (5)
	3. C Martin (6)
	4. Q Griffin (7)
	5. T Bell
WR	1. T Holt (2)
	2. C Johnson (3)
	3. R Wayne (8)
	4. D Stallworth
TE	1. A Gates (15)
K	1. J Elam
	2. R Longwell
D	1. Dolphins

Looking at the above draft and think about what you see…

Alright, first off I won a championship with taking a quarterback in the first round. I had ranked my running backs and I had a line drawn after 6 franchise backs in my personal rankings. They were all gone by the time I drafted and so was Peyton Manning. This still left me with a franchise QB available and several franchise wide receiver's available.

In the second and third rounds people were already starting to reach for running backs and I went with the next best franchise player available in Tory Holt (Randy Moss almost slid to me), and I followed that with C Johnson. Three rounds and I still had no RB. I knew Tiki Barber and Curtis Martin were still sitting out there and in a combination league these guys would perform.

In the fourth round I started my own personal run on running backs. I selected Barber knowing he was the number one guy in a conservative (Coach Tom Coughlin) running offense. I then took my first sleeper C Brown as I knew he would be the starter based on predraft preparation and finally closed my dash on running backs, C Martin. I had three starting running backs, two #1 receivers and a franchise Quarterback. The following rounds I filled in looking for depth.

I selected Reggie Wayne with my 8th pick. Based on our rankings criteria great offense, great QB, indoor games, offensive coach (Coordinator Jack Burns) lots of points.

I took a kicker early enough before the run started and got one of the best in Elam.

Defense was taken at the end of the draft and so was TE. Antonio Gates was the last pick of my team. Lucky? Or did I do the research and know he was going to be the starter. I made an educated pick as was the case with WR Michael Jackson of Baltimore in 1996.

This was a low maintenance team and I rode this team to a 10-4 record. I rolled thru the playoffs and had another championship under my belt. The only player in my starting lineup during week 17 that I didn't draft was the Cardinals defense. I used weekly favorable match up play with picking up and dropping defenses as discussed earlier.

This was a good solid team which shows you that being prepared, picking franchise players when available, and following your rankings while drafting can produce the coveted hardware, satisfaction and enjoyment that being number one gives one.

A championship the hard way

The second of my championships was a much more difficult journey and thus more rewarding. Keep in mind when playing Fantasy Football, until you are officially eliminated (Black Tuesday) you still are only one move away baby.

Our league is a 12 team league based on a combination scoring. 6 points for any touchdown including passing, rushing, and receiving. 3 points for over 100 yards rushing or receiving with 2 points for every 50 over 100. Passing was 3 points for over 300 yards passing and 1 point for every 50 yards over 300. Field goals were 3 points under 50, 5 points over. Defense was basic 1 point per pick, 1 point per sack, 6 points per touchdown. 10 points for a shutout.

It is a 12 Team league with 3 divisions, division winners are in and then 3 wild cards. The best 2 teams get a bye in week 15 and the championship is week 17.

Our transactions were limited to one move per week unless your player shows up on the injury report. If you have one player or multiple players on the injury report (Thursday's paper) you could make the necessary moves to field a starting lineup.

This would affect the draft in that you couldn't afford to have too many players on bye regardless of position. If they weren't hurt, you could only make one move.

We use a serpentine draft, 14 rounds, with pick #1 starting the first round and ending the second (24th pick), and starting the third (25th).

For the first time ever I got the number one pick of the draft. Now think about scoring in this league for a minute. Touchdowns passes are 6 points making Culpepper and Peyton Manning very attractive.

I however went with the player at his position that was consistently head and tails above everyone else for the last 2 years. Priest Holmes.

Here is the rest of my draft and the round in parenthesis I took the player in:

QB 1. Bulger (5)
2. C Palmer (10)
RB 1. P Holmes (1)
2. C Brown (3)
3. Barlow (4)
4. Q Griffin (9)
WR 1. H Ward (2)
2. J McCareins (6)
3. D Stallworth (7)
4. Q Morgan (11)
5. J Gage (12)
6. R Woods (14)
K 1. J Brown (8)
D 1. Buffalo (13)

Looking at this draft you would think, how did you win a championship with a draft like this? That is what makes this case study different from the first. In the first case study we drafted well and it was low maintenance all year. This is the opposite however I had a huge start with Priest Holmes as the man.

Let's start by looking at round by round, breakdown and the thinking during the draft.

Round one was Priest and I didn't even hesitate. People passed on Priest last year in our league, and his owner has had won the title the second year in a row.

When my pick came around again with two in a row, the running backs had been picked fairly clean and the top receivers were starting to go. I had Hines Ward as a consistent 10-14 TD high *golden boy* performer so I grabbed him. This would give me a player to pencil in every week at wide out.

I then went with another RB as I wanted to make sure I had another solid starter on a high scoring team. With Eddie George moving on to Dallas, my preseason scouting had shown that Chris Brown was going to be the number one guy. Tennessee was a good offensive team that had traditionally produced 1000 yard rusher and double digit scorers.

By round four and five I was looking for a QB, and a for sure starter at the RB position. Bulger had good potential with no Warner looking over his shoulder and two studs for receivers. He also had a back that could catch with hall of famers, and a coach who was an offense genius. However, I was a little concerned about Pace not signed and a beat up offensive line.

Barlow was rated high in all of the fantasy books and he was a for sure starter. I figured I could get some spot starts from him and go with my first two backs.

Round six and seven was filling in receiver depth with number 1 and 2 starters. Round eight, I got the kicker of my choice as I felt Seattle was going to have a huge year.

Round 9-12 was filling in depth and backups. I drafted Griffin convinced he had the job and could become another Shanahan 1000-yard rusher protégée. Palmer was a sleeper at QB since he beat out a solid J Kitna, and had some decent offensive weapons in the Johnson's and Warrick.

Round 13, I took my defense, and in 14 since we do not need to draft a TE, I used a sleeper pick at wide out. Boy did this guy sleep. ZZZZ.

At the start of the year, I was happy with my depth at RB, all starters. I had on my team a decent QB, and a little weak at receiver, with one good starter. This would be an area to upgrade thru trades with my RB depth and free agency. I also needed to make sure my backup QB panned out. With 6 points for a TD pass, QB will consistently score you the most points based on that and a high injury rate position you need to have two good ones.

Week 1 came and we were ready to go to battle. My team "In the Zone" was playing "The Good Fellas" a division game. As explained earlier I did not make any moves and went with whom I drafted. Week number 1 went like this:

	In The Zone		Good Fellas	
QB	Bulger	6	McNair	6
RB	Q Griffin	23	M Faulk	5
	P Holmes	23	Tomlinson	9
WR	J McCareins	0	Ferguson	0
	D Stallworth	0	A Johnson	0
	H Ward	0	S Moss	0
K	J Brown	3	D Akers	7
D	Bills	4	Tampa	6

In The Zone 59 Good Fellas 33

I had been sweating this one out going into Sunday nights match up of Kansas City vs. Denver. I needed 3 Td's and over 100 yards from one of my backs to get the win. I knew it was always possible whenever Kansas City's defense was involved. I also had a guy named Holmes, I was feeling good he would score but the question was how many?

On the bench, I had a TD from Q Morgan, and Carson Palmer who had thrown 2. Chris Brown went over 100 yards rushing in his debut and was looking like the real deal.

Looking at what my team had done initially, I still wanted to upgrade at wide out. A Gates was intriguing to me as was the rookie Roy Williams who I actually asked about in the draft, but took R Woods instead. Oops!

The waiver system in this league is based on the team that scores the least amount of fantasy points in the previous week's game. Both of these players went to other teams so I grabbed Lamar Gordon the RB in Miami for R Woods. You can never have too many backs. Week 2 was another divisional match up.

In the Zone			Red Rockers	
QB	Bulger	6	A Brooks	18
RB	Griffin	0	A Green	3
	Holmes	6	R Johnson	0
WR	McCareins	0	P Warrick	0
	Stallworth	9	T Glenn	0
	H Ward	11	P Price	0
K	J Brown	4	Jano	7
D	Buff	2	Miami	6

In the Zone 38 Red Rockers 34

I sweated thru the Miami vs. Cincinnati game Sunday night and I had another win. My record was 2-0 baby. See how Fantasy Football can make an exciting football game out of two struggling teams like Miami vs. Cinncy.

Q Griffin had laid and egg after the strong start but you cannot score every week can you? Stallworth proved a good counter play to his Aaron Brooks as I had thought about starting Q Morgan until he started Brooks.

My bench play at running back was strong with Barlow scoring 15 that week against New Orleans and C Brown coming up with 150+ yards and a TD. Backup QB had done nothing and I was less then impressed watching Lamar Gordon on the tube.

We can make only one transaction a week unless someone is on the injury report so I made my one move, dropped Buffalo D on the bye, and picked up NY Giants.

Week 3 the last of the divisional match ups until the end of the season and the first of the bye weeks.

	In the Zone		Wolverines	
QB	Bulger	18	Carr	6
RB	C Brown	9	C Portis	0
	Q Griffin	0	D Davis	0
WR	Q Morgan	6	A Lelie	6
	Stallworth	0	A Bryant	0
	H Ward	6	T Gonzalez	9
K	J Brown	10	J Wilkins	7
D	NY Giants	5	Philly	5

In the Zone 54 Wolverines 33

I had just made it thru the divisional round for the first time with a perfect 3-0 record and was in first place. Divisional games were also the first tiebreaker; the season was looking good however, I still needed to address some issues.

Was Q Griffin a temporary success or was KC's defense that horrendous against the run? Was McCareins ever going to catch some passes, let alone catch a TD? C Palmer is looking like a rookie.

Week 4 transactions, I need to address my kicker bye and L Gordon is hurt so I can make two moves. No other RB in Miami thrills me and I need help at wide out. Reche Caldwell is showing up in my box scores and getting the ball with 2 TDs. P Dawson has showed up on my Wednesday leader board in kicker scoring with 17 pts and Cleveland is at home. There are a few other kickers out there but I pickup Dawson and Caldwell.

Week 4 we begin our outside the division match ups. I go against a guy who fails to call in his lineup. (Remember tip earlier, call in lineup early to deal with your byes, fine tune with your injury report after Thursday).

	In The Zone		Big Daddy	
QB	Bulger	6	Brady	12

RB	Barlow	0	S Alexander	0
	Holmes	15	E Smith	15
WR	H Ward	0	I Bruce	3
	Q Morgan	0	K Johnson	0
	D Stallworth	0	K Robinson	0
K	P Dawson	5	Gramatica	7
D	N Y Giants	2	Seattle	0

Big Daddy 37 In the Zone 28
I got beat! Ouch! This is beyond frustrating; my wide outs are pathetic. If I play my new pickup Reche Caldwell, I have a tie game as he scores 9. That is all right I am still in first place at 3-1.

I do not like my wide outs and I have been watching Michael Clayton from Tampa get the ball and score. However, we can only make one move a week and with passing TD's worth 6, I have to address my backup QB situation.

C Palmer had a nice first week where he threw 2 but he is getting his jersey colors confused and tossing picks, with no more TD's yet. D Bress has 6 TD's and he is on the leader board. I pull the trigger on Brees. Antonio Gates is turning into a Gonzalez like TE, and I have Reche Caldwell for the hookup. San Diego is also winning and looking like a surprise team in the West.

The league has its first trade of the year and a drop of sweat rolls down my furrowed brow. Some pressure has been applied on my team early and my number one rival in the division has just landed Chad Johnson for Marshall Faulk. This looks like a solid deal for the Good Fellas as Marshall is fading and he already has Tomlinson and Dunn. Week 5

	In The Zone		Big Dogs	
QB	Bulger	27	Culpepper	34
RB	Barlow	0	C Dillon	0
	C Brown	15	F Taylor	0
WR	J McCareins	0	L Coles	0
	H Ward	0	D Mason	6
	R Caldwell	0	A Toomer	0
K	P Dawson	11	Elam	8
D	N Y Giants	3	Atlanta	3

In The Zone 56 Big Dogs 51

4-1 overall and rolling along. Beat Daunte and his 5 TD tosses. This is the second time this year that Big Dogs has gotten 5 TDS from Daunte and lost. Bulger is consistently getting TD's and my kicker had a big game. On the bench, Brees has thrown 2 TD's and looking more and more like the real deal. Wide receivers are a joke and Quentin Griffin should have been traded while he had value. I have to do something to get wide out production. I begin to send out trade feelers. P Holmes has gone thru the bye.

Transactions: I look at Droughns but he is snatched up and I go with changing D's for the 3rd time. I grab the Jets and drop J Gage. Who?

Week 6

	In the Zone		The Hitmen	
QB	Bulger	12	Bledsoe	6
RB	Barlow	6	S Davis	0
	Holmes	6	McAllister	12
WR	Stallworth	0	Curry	0
	Ward	0	Holt	15
	R Caldwell	0	Moulds	0
K	P Dawson	10	Carney	7
D	N Y Jets	4	St Louis	9

The Hit men49 In the Zone 38

I was hanging in there until Monday night. Torry Holt and St Louis D stick a fork in me. Michael Clayton looked good again. I need to get him on the squad. McCareins has yet to score this year, and Hines Ward has now become a secondary target with the quarterback change in Pittsburg. Hines Ward is officially a bust, and I am looking to start making some deals.

Michael Clayton is picked up for the Jets D. In addition, Reche Caldwell goes down for the year so we go with Brandon Lloyd a #1 wide out to try to fix our receiver position. Another trade is commenced; Rod Gardner goes for Javon Walker. I would have liked to get a piece of Walker, as he is a stud. I need a receiver!

The perspiration is staining my shirts as I toss and turn at night. It is 3:30 am and my wife wakes me up at night to ask who are Owens, Harrison and Stokley. Kick in Ass who trades for Walker is looking formidable with the Farve to Walker hookup. He also has Moss and Gates.

Week 7

	In the Zone		B Squad	
QB	Bulger	12	McNabb	28
RB	C Brown	0	Zereoue	0
	Holmes	27	T Jones	6
WR	Clayton	6	Givens	3
	McCareins	0	Horn	3
	Q Morgan	0	Owens	15
K	P Dawson	7	Vandy	6
D	N Y Giants	3	Minnesota	5

B Squad 66 In the Zone 55

I get instant production from the Clayton pickup. Watching the ticker on the tube I launch from my seat four times as Priest Holmes crosses the stripe. I feel so confident I call and talk smack to B-Squad. However, the hookup angle comes up big for B Squad with the McNabb to Owens combo. This was a tough loss.

I fall to 4-3 and out of first place in my

division. My team has been consistent in scoring and I still hold the 3-0 divisional tie breaker.

Going into week 8 I am ready to make a major deal to improve my wider receiver position. While scouting other teams, I talk with The Hitmen and their depth at wide out. They need a running back for this week and are ready to deal. I trade Chris Brown for Torry Holt. Priest Holmes and Kevin Barlow have both gotten thru the byes and Brown continues to come out at half time during games.

In other transactions, I pick up K Brown Houston's kicker for J McCareins and Jonathan Wells for the injured Quentin Griffin. There is also a trade as The Hitmen trades Byron Leftwich for Michael Vick.

Week 8, I am playing the Commish. I catch a break as Moss is still out hurt.

	In The Zone		Kickin Ass	
QB	Brees	30	Farve	8
RB	Barlow	0	Levens	0
	Holmes	21	K Jones	6
WR	Q Morgan	0	J Walker	6
	H Ward	0	A Gates	12
	B Lloyd	0	E Johnson	0
K	K Brown	8	Scobee	6
D	N Y Giants	2	New Eng	0

In the Zone 61 Kickin Ass 38

St Louis was on the bye so I did not get a chance to preview my new hookup combo. It is time now to start looking at the injury protection angle. Priest is the franchise and Derrick Blaylock has scored a few TD's and looks like a solid backup should Priest go down.

I also have entertained trade offers with the Wolverines as he is looking for a wide out. Clinton Portis and Domanick Davis have for sale signs. I quickly offer up H Ward for D Davis. This is on Wards reputation alone as with the change in QB to Roethlisberger and the fountain of youth in Jerome Bettis, Hines is a has been. The Wolverines get a much better offer and deal Portis for J Horn from the B Squad. This is a solid deal for both clubs.

I for go protecting my player this week and pickup Willie Green from Cleveland. The player that teases everyone with his ability but rarely translates into points. I hope Priest doesn't get hurt.

Week 9. I take on the league Juggernaut. The Mudsharks have the best QB and backfield in the league. On the Mudsharks bench is C Martin and J Bettis. He could use an upgrade at wide out but nobody has been able to get one of the backs.

	In the Zone		Mudsharks	
QB	Bulger	12	Manning	24

RB	Barlow	6	Barber	12
	Holmes	6	E James	3
WR	Clayton	0	D Jackson	15
	H Ward	12	Galloway	0
	Holt	9	Shockey	6
K	Dawson	9	Stover	13
D	N Y Giants	5	Denver	4

Mudsharks 77 In the Zone 59

A couple of things happen this week. I went back and forth with my QB and Brees is on my bench with 24 points. How did D Jackson score 15 points in a game? Answer: The 49ers D.

Priest Holmes goes down this week but the extent of the injury is said to be a sprain knee. Insomnia returns as I did not take out a policy on Holmes and scored 59 points putting me near the end of the waiver list. Nobody is convinced Priest is out for long and I land Blaylock on waivers for J Wells. Another nice move made on the waiver wire late was B Griese being picked up, a serviceable QB in week 10 on the waiver wire. Subzero is paying attention to late season upgrades.

Week 10

In the Zone			Sub Zero	
QB	Bulger	6	Griese	12
RB	Barlow	12	Lewis	0
	Blaylock	11	O Smith	6
WR	Clayton	6	Gardner	0

	Ward	0	McDonald	0
	Holt	0	J Smith	0
K	Dawson	4	Rackers	5
D	N Y Giants	2	Baltimore	6

In The Zone 41 Sub Zero 38

My record is now 6-4 with four games to play. Blaylock has paid off instantly and B Lloyd has scored 2 weeks in a row sitting on the pine.

I am tired of my pathetic defense (I cannot play every weekly match up because of the one free agent rule) putting up paltry numbers and I upgrade with Pittsburg for the N Y Giants.

Week 11

	In the Zone		The Swarm	
QB	D Brees	12	Green	16
RB	Barlow	0	Suggs	0
	Blaylock	0	Westbrook	12
WR	Clayton	0	Branch	9
	Ward	0	Muhammad	15
	Holt	0	R Smith	0
K	K Brown	7	Andersen	2
D	Pittsburg	12	Dallas	1

The Swarm 55 In the Zone 37

There is nothing to say about this loss, just a bad week. The Swarm has a good team with a few starters out this week. A foreshadow of things to come.

I do not have confidence with the mess in San Francisco and Kevin Barlow. After highlighting players week after week and checking the injury reports to see which backs are hurt. I come up with Nick Goings. The Carolina running back had a huge week before in Arizona, as another back went down for the panthers.

Week 12

	In the Zone		Wolverines	
QB	Bulger	17	Carr	12
RB	Blaylock	12	Droughns	9
	Goings	3	Davis	9
WR	Clayton	0	Stokley	18
	Ward	0	Lelie	0
	Holt	0	Horn	11
K	K Brown	7	Wilkins	5
D	Pittsburg	6	Philly	7

Wolverines 71 In the Zone 45

In the Zone falls to 6-6 and has now suffered its first divisional loss, a crucial tiebreaker. This week was particularly depressing being the Thanksgiving Week with games on Thursday. Stokley had 3 TD's before the turkey and stuffing were on the table. After that, it was a chase the whole weekend.

Priest Holmes is still questionable. Looking ahead at possible playoff match ups, Nate Kaeding has been lighting it up with the San Diego offense and their schedule looks great for weeks 15-17. I drop K Brown to pickup Nate. My team has consistently putting up 40+ points a game, yet has not clinched.

Week 13

	In the Zone		Red Rockers	
QB	Bulger	0	Brooks	18
RB	Blaylock	6	Green	0
	Goings	9	R Johnson	0
WR	Clayton	0	Colbert	0
	Ward	6	Porter	6
	Holt	11	Boldin	0
K	Kaeding	8	J Brown	7
D	Pittsburg	2	N Y Jets	4

In the Zone 42 Red Rockers35

This is a huge divisional win. I did not counter with Stallworth this time as the player I would have benched was H Ward. Bulger had the 0, as he got hurt. Nooo! Sprained shoulder, augh!

Here is where depth comes into play. I have Brees and his match ups look good. I need to make a move at QB and Bulgers backup Chandler does not appeal to me. I also want to protect Blaylock as L Johnson is getting some carries and looking good.

Scouring the wire, we come up with C Palmer for Bulger this week, Larry Johnson for

B Lloyd. Barlow is out with a concussion and I am dying for receiver help. I pickup A Crumpler.

It is do or die this week and if I win, I am in. I still can lose and have enough tiebreakers to get in. I am playing the number one team in my division. There are also two other teams playing within the division facing elimination. There is a lot of tension and excitement going into the last regular season weekend with the division schedule format discussed in the previous chapter.

Week 14

	In the Zone		Good Fellas	
QB	Brees	12	Plummer	0
RB	Blaylock	6	Dunn	3
	Goings	9	Tomlinson	9
WR	Ward	0	A Johnson	0
	Holt	11	M Robinson	0
	Crumpler	0	C Johnson	6
K	Kaeding	7	Akers	5
D	Pittsburg	3	Tampa Bay	4

In the Zone 48 Good Fellas 27

We are in! Awesome. Finish with an 8-6 record, 5-1 in the division. Overall, I have clinched the number 4 seed. Let the playoffs begin. The last piece of business is setting your roster for the playoffs.

In most leagues you can't make a move once

the playoffs start so you need to make sure that you have solid backups that can play if your guys go down to injury.

I wait until the injury report comes out to get clarification on multiple positions. Carson Palmer has an injured ACL and is too much of a question mark to play. Bulger has been upgrade to questionable and he was my starter and hookup to begin with. I grab Bulger.

M Hicks is taking carries in San Francisco with Barlow's injury and I finally drop P Holmes to give me some depth in the backfield. Lastly, the Buffalo defense has caught fire and looking ahead at their match ups of at Cinncy, at San Francisco and at home in a possible must win (for the Bills) game against Pittsburg. I dump Pittsburg D and pickup Buffalo.

My roster is set for the playoffs and I like my chances. My team is consistently scoring points and I cannot meet the number one seed until the finals based on our format.

Divisional Playoffs: The Mudsharks, and B Squad get the first round byes and I match up against Big Daddy who put the big hurt on me earlier this year.

In the Zone			Big Daddy	
QB	Brees	6	Brady	18
RB	Goings	6	Alexander	0

	L Johnson	17	E Smith	0
WR	Clayton	0	Bruce	0
	Ward	3	Burleson	15
	Holt	0	K Johnson	6
K	Kaeding	3	Gramatica	0
D	Buffalo	17	Seattle	0

In the Zone 52 Big Daddy 39
I had a nice big lead going into Monday night but Brady scored early and it left me biting my nails Every time New England got in the Red Zone, I dug out a Corey Dillon jersey and was screaming, "give it to Dillon" until my voice went hoarse.

Victory tastes so sweet and the moves towards the end of the season are paying off. Buffalo had a huge game and Larry Johnson running behind the big KC line is producing big. This guy should be on everyone's list next year.

In week 16 the semifinals, I match up against the number 2 seed. B Squad. He has some issues with Philadelphia clinching the home field thru out and Owens out with the ankle. McNabb might see only a limited role and he has a lack of depth with Rattay as his backup. I have my own issues with Bulger out, however my depth is paying off with a match up between the Brees led Chargers and Indianapolis. The potential is there for a high scoring affair.

	In the Zone		B Squad	
QB	Brees	18	McNabb	6
RB	Goings	3	Portis	0
	L Johnson	12	T Jones	3
WR	Stallworth	6	Givens	0
	Ward	0	Kennison	0
	Holt	0	Hakim	0
K	Kaeding	9	Vanderjagt	14
D	Buffalo	6	Minnesota	8

In the Zone 54 B Squad 31

The Monday Night Game between the Eagles and Rams had us both tuned in on the edge of our seats. Madden and Michaels were talking about how long McNabb should play and I know I had my answer. He played the first series, went right down the field, and scored. That was it for McNabb and that was the ballgame. Depth at QB played a huge role in this game. I had to play my backup due to injury and B Squad had to play McNabb and hope for the best.

The Championship: The number one seed has been knocked off and I am playing The Swarm a 6 seed. I am playing the hottest team in the league with the two hottest players in the league, Mushin Muhammad and Willis McGahee. I am facing the dilemma my opponent faced last game in that I have a team that has clinched everything in San Diego and that QB probably wont play much, if at all. I have only one option at QB, however looking ahead at the beginning of the year I knew this would be a good match up. The "greatest show on Turf" at home has to win to make the playoffs and I have two of their starters.

	In the Zone		The Swarm	
QB	Bulger	24	Green	10
RB	Goings	0	McGahee	12
	L Johnson	15	L Suggs	3
WR	Clayton	6	Harrison	6
	Ward	0	Smith	0
	Holt	15	Muhammad	12
K	Kaeding	6	Andersen	4
D	Buffalo	10	Dallas	2

In the Zone 76 The Swarm 49

I have won the CHAMPIONSHIP! This is the second one this year, 3rd in the last 3 years, and 5th overall. The system works.

Review and Summary

Lesson #1-Before beginning your fantasy football season, it is important to develop the fantasy mindset. Fantasy Football happens year round. Free Agency in the beginning of March, the draft in April and training camp starts in late July (which means injuries). The first preseason games where position battles are won are in August and the season begins after Labor Day.

Publications will begin showing up in July and August in anticipation of everyone's fantasy draft. Remember to pickup 2-3 of these magazines and make sure they cover the key areas as discussed in Lesson #1.

Also, use the web sites listed in the Appendix to help assemble all your online information as it becomes available.

Lesson #2-Interpret the information to develop your own rankings. To begin this process make sure you have read your draft publications from cover to cover. Couple this data with the current online and training camp news from Newspapers, USA today, and USA Today Sports Weekly and you will begin to have a clear picture of who is getting the rock. Do your own rankings on players in your own notebook for the draft. Write them down drawing lines in-between the *franchise players, golden boys, and players with potential.*

Rank these players according to each of the position breakdowns we discussed in this chapter.

Lesson #3-The Draft. Stay true to your rankings and pick from them. You have done the research; it does not matter when people will say, "He was 45th in my magazine". These rankings will keep you focused during the draft. Pick the highest valued player on the board. Do not draft a team full of sleepers or rookies. Defense and Tight ends should be picked last unless you are getting Gonzalez or Gates.

Lesson #4-Managing your team is not over after the draft. There are plenty of players every year that get a chance to start due to injury or lack of production. Keep updated on the latest information online or by reading the NFL notes in your local newspaper. Injury reports will also give you much needed info on starter's status. Going back to your fantasy magazines and look at the depth chart to select backups who may well turn out to be studs. Keep your weekly box scores and read them every week. Highlight free agents so you can keep track of them. Make sure to update your binder on players being dropped.

Lesson #5-Who should I start? There are many different resources available to help you improve your odds of selecting a winning lineup. Make sure you field a lineup that is on the field every week. Injuries and byes are part of the game and you need to have a plan. There is plenty of information available to help you break down each individual match up and use the points in this chapter, to help you field a competitive lineup.

Lesson #6-Even if you already know how to play Fantasy Football it does not hurt to read this chapter. I have been in quite a few different leagues over the years and everyone has their nuances. In my research, I learned of more fun and entertaining ways to play the game, I enjoy. You might find some optional rules here that will help your league.

Lesson #7-A Case Study, A Championship Season. The key points of the first championship were; I took a franchise quarterback in the first round, and I did not select a running back until the fourth round. I drafted the best available players and was not sucked into the early run on running backs especially after the franchise and golden boys were gone.

The second championship was a year of constantly pounding the waiver wire, and making a key trade to upgrade my team. I rotated my QB's backs effectively and used injury protection to help with my #1 running back going down. I upgraded both my starters and backups to help in the case of injuries and it paid off in the end.

Appendix I

2005 Free Agency

Quarterbacks

QB-**Jeff Garcia** from Cleveland to Detroit. I like this signing. It has all the ingredients of a good one if Garcia can stay healthy and earn starting job. Old coach who is familiar with Jeff's game and a plethora of up and coming receivers to work with like Rodgers, Williams (both), and M Pollard. Detroit should be a team on the rise. +

QB-**Kurt Warner** from NY Giants to Arizona. I like this one as long as the Cards are winning as he has signed a one-year deal. Good offensive coach, 2 solid receivers in Boldin and Fitzgerald. Cards play in a division with terrible pass defenses, the NFC west. Kurt also has intangibles; the Giants were winning before he got the hook. +

QB-**Kelly Holcomb** from Cleveland to Buffalo. Kelly had a great one game run last year in Cleveland and can play a little. Watch to see how this race for the starting position shakes out. +/-

QB-**Trent Dilfer** from Seattle to Cleveland. Trent signed a four-year deal, which pretty much makes him the starter at this point. Cleveland is a terrible team, with a new coach. The addition of Reuben Droughns and the drafting of WR Braylon Edwards help their cause. Trent could be a serviceable number 2 fantasy quarterback. I do not expect too much out of him this year, however Cleveland should score more points then last year. -/+

Running Backs

RB **Lamont Jordan** from the Jets to Oakland. Lamont is a running back with potential that has always had to take a back seat to Curtis Martin. He will have a chance to shine in Oakland with no clear number one back at this point. +

RB **Derrick Blaylock** from KC to Jets. This helps sort out the Priest Holmes situation a little. Blaylock still looks to be locked into a pass catching 3rd down back. Has good value if Martin gets hurt. He scored 9 times last year. +/-

RB **Ron Dayne** from NY Giants to Denver. Mike Shanahan made Rueben Droughts a 1000 yard rusher. You never know. Sleeper pick. Watch depth charts. -/-

Wide Receivers

WR **David Terrell** from Chicago to New England.

Terrell is a highly underachieving player who in the right system might produce. He will be behind Givens and Branch but definitely worth a flyer as a later round pick. Change of scenery could rectify career. Anybody who goes from the Bears to the Patriots gets a plus. +

WR **Derrick Mason** from Tennessee to Baltimore. Who is going to throw him the ball? Mason has never been an above average touchdown guy 5, 9, 5 and 7. I don't see anything better on this run first, and then kick a field goal team of Baltimore. +/-

WR **Plaxico Burress** from Pittsburg to New York Giants. He becomes the instant number one receiver in New York and their new deep threat. This will probably mean the end for Toomer. Plaxico has no proven QB at this point and the whole team will be a question mark on offense other than Tiki. He is worth a look as a third or fourth receiver but will probably be drafted way too early. -/+

WR **David Patten** from New England to Redskins. He should be a 2nd - 3rd wide out again. Washington is a horrible offense, with a question mark at quarterback. Might want to get a couple of pictures with that Lombardi trophy, could be awhile. -

WR **Laveranues Coles** from Washington to NY Jets out of Washington can't be a bad thing. Caught 90 balls for 950 yds and 1 TD. Didn't the Redskins only score like 10 all year? It can't get any worse. +

WR **Santana Moss** from NY Jets to Washington. There isn't any Thiesman throwing the rock. Ugh. Moss was a major disappointment last year however came on late. Finished with 45 receptions, 838 yards and 5 TD's. He leaves a poor throwing offense for an anemic one. -

WR **Travis Taylor** from Baltimore to Minnesota. Who? No quarterback in Baltimore, however this guy hasn't shown anything. The plus side is high powered offense, Kelly Campbell's legal problems, great quarterback. He could be a sleeper. Keep an eye on during training camp to see where he winds up on the depth chart. -/+

TE **Marcus Pollard** from Indy to Detroit. He went from Indy to Detroit, from Peyton Manning to Joey Harrington. The signing of an experience quarterback like Garcia might help a veteran like Pollard. -

Appendix II

2005 Trades and Rookies

WR **Randy Moss**-Traded from Minnesota to Oakland. As discussed at the beginning of the book this should not affect Moss's production. Collins is no Culpepper but Moss made Gus Frerotte look like a Pro Bowler. Moss should easily score 15+ TD's if he stays healthy.

RB **Reuben Droughns**-traded from Denver to Cleveland. Rueben now falls into the abysmal offense of Cleveland. His value definitely goes down as he went from Denver which produces 1000+ yard backs like a normal day at work, to the Browns. Reuben looks like he will be splitting carries again. Lee Suggs's value goes down for the same reason and this all but assures Willie Green is gone. Watch in training camp to see if they name a number one guy. The interesting part of this deal is that Denver has handed their job over to Tatum Bell. Quentin Griffin looks like a 3rd down back and Bell will be the man. --

The Rookies

In this section we will list some of the rookies selected in the draft that play one of the eight scoring positions. We will talk about the first round picks and touch on selected others (round picked in parenthesis) that we feel are notable at this point. Keep in mind this publication has went to press in May and the purpose of this section is to familiarize you with the players, destinations, and how they fit in at this point in time. All rookies need to be evaluated during training camp and you should be looking online and in the newspapers for updated information on who is winning the starting jobs. Some of these players will not even make their teams.

Quarterbacks

Alex Smith, Utah 6-3, 212 lbs. (1) San Francisco- Alex plays a position that rarely has immediate impact in fantasy football. Looking back last year Eli Manning played and was a nonfactor fantasy wise. It will be interesting to see if they turn the reigns immediately over to Smith as Rattay and Dorsey don't look like the answer and the franchise is years away. If Alex plays right away he has a pro bowl caliber tight end in Eric Johnson. His receiving corps is Brandon Lloyd who looks legitimate and the aging Curtis Conway with 2nd year sleeper candidate Rashaun Woods waiting in the wings. If the Niners could get solid production from their offensive line to help Hicks and Barlow establish a running game, Alex Smith might have some success. Being the number one pick in the NFL draft, he has all the physical tools to be a performer in the NFL however we all know it takes more than that. He is not worth picking in the draft unless San Francisco commits to him being the clear cut starter for the whole year. At most he is a 2nd or 3rd quarterback on any fantasy roster.

Aaron Rodgers, California 6-1, 223 lbs. (1) Green Bay-a polished QB who ran a more pro style offense. Is locked in behind Brett Farve for a year and would probably only see time if an injury were to occur. A nonfactor for fantasy players however Packer fans have to be tickled a kid ranked this high slid to them.

Jason Campbell, Auburn 6-4, 223 lbs. (1) Washington-Patrick Ramsey was named the starter and it is his job to lose. Fortunately for Jason we have heard that about Patrick before. Campbell could conceivably play after the Redskins are eliminated from the playoff hunt or Ramsey goes belly up. Speaking on the Redskins offense ...well.... Alright they have Clinton Portis and he can't possibly be as mediocre as he was last year. Can he? Campbell has no immediate fantasy value. Keep an eye on him late in the year.

Running Backs

Ronnie Brown, Auburn 6-0, 233 lbs. (1) Miami- Brown is an immediate impact player on a team desperate for a go to guy. He comes into a new offense with a new coordinator Scott Linneahan from the Vikings. Brown will see the ball rushing and thru the air increasing chance for potential for scoring as he is a polished pass receiver. He should be an every down back with the potential for 7+ TD's. I still think Miami is a few years away from the playoffs and they play in a division with tough defenses, with New England, Buffalo, and New York. However being the second worst team in the league the Fish should get a very favorable schedule. I would select him as your 3rd running back option with spot starts during the year with favorable match ups. He could merit a 2nd running back slot if the crop of starters is bare and everyone on offense comes back healthy in Miami.

Chris Benson, Texas 5-10, 222 lbs. (1) Chicago- Benson is a workhorse and durable. He carried the ball 250+ times per year in 3 years of heavy use in college. Not as fast as Brown and Williams but as a nose for the goal line. A good receiver and solid blocker keeps him on the field in third down situations. The question now is what does Chicago do with it's two other backs. A Train is probably gone and my initial reaction is combined carries with Thomas Jones, every fantasy owner's nightmare. This deserves watching in training camp to determine who is named number one. Chicago still has a horrendous offense but have upgraded at receiver with M Muhammad. If Benson is named the starter he should be a 2 or 3 back.

Carnell (Cadillac) Williams, Auburn 5-11, 217 lbs. (1) Tampa Bay-There are some questions on his pass catching, and pass blocking ability. There also have been questions about his strength moving the pile and his durability. Our question is with these deficiencies how he will get significant PT to make an impact. Mike Pittman is effective at catching the ball out of the backfield and Alstott can move the pile. What does Cadillac do? It sounds an awful lot like a 3 headed monster in Tampa Bay. Watch depth chart projections in your publications to see where Cadillac fits in. If Pittman is moved he becomes the starter and worth a pick as a number 3 or 4 back. You still always have the goal line vulture Mike Alstott in Tampa Bay, when he is healthy.

J.J. Arrington, California 5-8, 214 lbs. (2) Arizona Arrington comes to a team with a proven offensive system but short on talent. They are upgrading the talent level and things look headed in the right direction under Coach Dennis Green. Arrington was a workhorse is his last year where he gained 2,018 against top notch competition. He is a little on the small side and initial fears are he would not be a goal line back. Marcel Shipp is currently the starter but Denny likes speed. As for rotating backs, last year Denny committed to Emmitt all year long. Emmitt posted decent fantasy numbers at the RB position and now has retired. Watch to see what Shipp's status is in his recovery from a broken leg. If Arrington is the man he becomes a number 3 or 4 back and worth a draft pick.

Eric Shelton, Louisville, (2) Carolina-Eric is a big kid who currently would be third on the depth chart behind Davis and Foster. Carolina had so many injuries at running back last year that Nick Goings ended up being the feature back at the end of the year. Carolina has a good system that produces 1000 yard rushers and featured scorers. Shelton is too far down the depth chart at this point to make an impact unless players in front of him are moved.

Maurice Clarett, Ohio State, (3) Denver-We have talked endlessly about Shanahan's ability to turn any back into a star. Tatum Bell looks like the man, but Clarett could be a goal line specialist. His selection by Denver is intriguing, so watch to see how he is used in preseason games.

Marion Barber III, Minnesota, (4) Dallas-Marion was a two time 1000 yard rusher in the Big Ten. Eddie George is gone; Marion is #2 on depth chart.

Ciatrick Fason, Florida, (4) Minnesota-Fason joins the stable of running backs in Minnesota however will be given a chance to win the job based on Bennett's inability to stay healthy and Onterio's history. A solid sleeper in a good offense.

Wide Receivers

Braylon Edwards, Michigan 6-3, 211 lbs. (1) Cleveland-the most polished receiver of the draft and put into a situation to be a rookie impact player. His competition is limited in Cleveland and he should be an immediate starter. Romeo comes over from New England to help install the Patriots balanced scoring attack and Cleveland is making moves to try and upgrade the offense to become more competitive. They have traded for Reuben Droughns and brought in a veteran at QB with Trent Dilfer. Also, Kellen Winslow will be back healthy to help keep the heat off of Edwards. I see Braylon catching 6+ TD passes and being a solid number 2 (depending on match ups) or 3 receiver. A 6-9th round pick watch your mock drafts to see where he goes.

Mike Williams, USC 6-5, 229 lbs. (1) Detroit-there are serious concerns about his lack of separation speed in the NFL. His size and raw ability should not be a problem in the red zone. Jump balls are the in thing and the bigger the mismatch the better. Mike will get plenty of these opportunities near the goal line in Detroit. The real question is will he be on the field for the rest of the game as Detroit has Roy Williams, Charles Rogers, and Tai Streets. He might become the new type of goal line vulture for receivers and come in during red zone plays. Rogers is talented but always hurt and if Mike isn't too rusty from a year off football he should see the field enough to have some impact as a rookie. Watch training camp reports to see how Charles Rogers, his direct competition comes back. Because right now Williams would behind him, the number 3 option in Detroit. A solid middle round receiver but don't pick him until after Roy Williams has been selected. Stock goes up if Jeff Garcia is named starter.

Troy Williamson, South Carolina 6-1, 203 lbs. (1)

Minnesota desperate for replacing Randy Moss's speed goes with Williamson in the draft instead of Williams. The Vikes already have a future star as a possession receiver in Nate Burleson. Marcus Robinson can be your goal line jump ball player. Williamson adds the vertical element that makes this offense so effective. He will have to prove he can be counted on to consistently produce as he came from a run orientated offense and does not have the gaudy college career stats. He becomes the 3rd option at wide receiver but comes into an offense that got production from all 3 spots last year. When your quarterback is as good as Daunte, you will have a chance to perform right away. The Vikings lost offense coordinator Scott Linneahan to Miami and promoted their offensive line coach who has no experience running an offense. The feeling here is the Vikes will have trouble scoring touchdowns this year. Williamson deserves consideration in the late rounds but not before Nate Burleson and Marcus Robinson has been drafted. A solid sleeper pick. Watch the training camp reports and depth charts as Kelly Campbell is the other burner used to stretch the field.

Matt Jones, Arkansas 6-6, 242 lbs. (1) Jacksonville-a converted quarterback who will play wide receiver or tight end. Look to see where he is listed at draft time as with his size and jumping ability he has more value at tight end and becomes a solid sleeper. He currently will be playing behind Reggie Williams and Jimmy Smith at wide out. Matt has outstanding speed but extremely raw. Watch depth charts to see where he ends up.

Mark Clayton, Oklahoma 5-10, 193 lbs. (1) Baltimore-could conceivably start right away across from Derrick Mason making him a number #2. He is a little on the small size for today's standards but makes up for it with speed. The problem in Baltimore continues to be the pass offense in general. This will be Kyle Boller's third year at the helm and should be his best. If he beats out the competition and is the number #2 option, watch your box scores early in the year to see if he is getting the ball and how the passing offense performs in Baltimore.

Rodney White, UAB 6-1, 201 lbs. (1) Atlanta-No mans land for wide receivers. The Falcons have no receivers that were worth anything fantasy wise except Alge Crumpler at tight end. The argument still can be made that this is a run first, Vick or Dunn or Duckett team and until they prove they have a passing game, pass on Falcon receivers. Watch to see where he ends up on the depth chart.

Peerless Price might be gone which would help and Michael Jenkins looks like he might develop into a solid player. Unless things change in Atlanta he has minimal draft value.

Reggie Brown, Georgia, (2) Philadelphia a 2nd rounder who could find immediate PT based on a continued lack of production from everyone not named TO.

Mark Bradley, Oklahoma, (2) Chicago, David Terrell is gone which leaves Muhsin Muhammad as the only penciled in starter. Chicago had the worst pass offense in the league last year. Bradley brings hope.

Roscoe Parrish, Miami (2) Buffalo-a burner, small in stature. Looks to be a third wide out or strictly return man.

Terrance Murphy, Texas A&M, (2) Green Bay, All Big 12 first team selection. He comes from the same school as Robert Ferguson. Terrance looks to be a kick, punt returner to start as he is miles down the depth chart at this point.

Vincent Jackson, Colorado, (2) San Diego-The chargers are looking for a receiver with Reche

Caldwell's status uncertain. Watch the depth charts to see if Jackson earns a starting job next to McCardell.
Courtney Roby, Indiana, (3) Tennessee-need to replace Mason.

Tight Ends

Heath Miller, Virginia 6-5, 256 lbs. (1) Pittsburg-Heath comes into a highly unfriendly tight end system in Pittsburg. Being a number #1 pick for the Steelers they will expect big things from him and his status deserves watching during training camp. If he earns the job another sleeper pick.

Kevin Everett, Miami, (3) Buffalo-He is from Miami.

Kickers

Mike Nugent, Ohio State, New York Jets-Surprising pick here for the Jets and it looks like Doug O Brien days are over. This 2nd round pick is an immediate impact player if he wins the job. The last two rookie kickers who landed jobs were Josh Brown in 2003 and Nick Kaeding in 2004. Both kickers booted 114 points locking them in as golden boy kickers. Take a for sure kicker first and Nugent would make a solid backup until he proves he can take over as your number one kicker.

Appendix III

Websites: Here are lists of websites that have fantasy football information on them. They contain everything from fantasy leagues, injury reports, advice, statistical services, to weekly lineup breakdowns. There are also many listings not written about here, just type in fantasy football and do a search.

Fanball.com
mockzone.com
CBSSportsline.com
ESPN.com
4for4.com
Allamerica.com
Fantasyfootballtoc.com
Sports.channel.aol.com (Aol users)
FantasyFootball.com
Bestbuy.com (leagues where you can win prizes)
fantasyfootball.usatoday.com
fantasyfootball-league.com
fantasyasylum.com
Sportingnews.com
Rototimes.com
FootballDiehards.com
footballsoftware.com
Fantasyfootballchallege.com
Fantasyfootballlessons.com (book website)

Appendix IV

Team Schedules

	8 Teams	10 Teams	12 Teams
Wk 1	1 vs. 5	10 vs. 9	1 vs. 2
	3 vs. 7	8 vs. 7	3 vs. 4
	2 vs. 6	1 vs. 2	5 vs. 6
	4 vs. 8	5 vs. 3	7 vs. 12
		6 vs. 4	8 vs. 11
			9 vs. 10
Wk 2	6 vs. 1	7 vs. 10	1 vs. 3
	8 vs. 3	9 vs. 6	2 vs. 4
	5 vs. 2	1 vs. 5	5 vs. 9
	7 vs. 4	4 vs. 2	6 vs. 10
		3 vs. 8	7 vs. 11
			8 vs. 12
Wk 3	1 vs. 7	8 vs. 9	1 vs. 4
	3 vs. 5	7 vs. 6	2 vs. 5
	2 vs. 8	2 vs. 3	3 vs. 6
	4 vs. 6	4 vs. 5	7 vs. 8
		10 vs. 1	9 vs. 12
			10 vs. 11

Wk 4	8 vs. 1	5 vs. 10	1 vs. 5
	6 vs. 3	8 vs. 1	2 vs. 6
	7 vs. 2	4 vs. 9	3 vs. 11
	5 vs. 4	7 vs. 2	4 vs. 12
		6 vs. 3	7 vs. 9
			8 vs. 10
Wk 5	1 vs. 3	9 vs. 10	1 vs. 6
	5 vs. 7	6 vs. 8	2 vs. 7
	2 vs. 4	2 vs. 1	3 vs. 9
	6 vs. 8	3 vs. 4	4 vs. 10
		5 vs. 7	5 vs. 11
			8 vs. 12
Wk 6	4 vs. 1	10 vs. 6	1 vs. 11
	8 vs. 5	7 vs. 8	2 vs. 10
	3 vs. 2	1 vs. 4	3 vs. 6
	7 vs. 6	3 vs. 5	4 vs. 5
		2 vs. 9	8 vs. 9
			7 vs. 12
Wk 7	1 vs. 2	4 vs. 10	1 vs. 12
	5 vs. 6	8 vs. 2	2 vs. 11
	3 vs. 4	1 vs. 9	3 vs. 8
	7 vs. 8	7 vs. 3	4 vs. 6
		5 vs. 6	5 vs. 9
			7 vs. 10

Wk 8	5 vs. 1	10 vs. 7	1 vs. 7
	7 vs. 3	9 vs. 8	2 vs. 8
	6 vs. 2	5 vs. 1	3 vs. 12
	8 vs. 4	3 vs. 2	4 vs. 9
		4 vs. 6	5 vs. 10
			6 vs. 11
Wk 9	1 vs. 6	8 vs. 10	1 vs. 8
	3 vs. 8	6 vs. 9	2 vs. 9
	2 vs. 5	1 vs. 3	3 vs. 7
	4 vs. 7	2 vs. 4	4 vs. 11
		7 vs. 5	5 vs. 12
			6 vs. 10
W10	7 vs. 1	6 vs. 10	1 vs. 10
	5 vs. 3	9 vs. 7	2 vs. 12
	8 vs. 2	4 vs. 1	3 vs. 5
	6 vs. 4	5 vs. 2	4 vs. 7
		8 vs. 3	6 vs. 9
			8 vs. 11
W11	1 vs. 8	3 vs. 10	1 vs. 9
	3 vs. 6	4 vs. 8	2 vs. 5
	2 vs. 7	5 vs. 9	3 vs. 10
	4 vs. 5	1 vs. 7	4 vs. 8
		2 vs. 6	6 vs. 12
			7 vs. 11

W12	3 vs. 1	10 vs. 2	1 vs. 4
	7 vs. 5	8 vs. 5	2 vs. 3
	4 vs. 2	9 vs. 3	5 vs. 8
	8 vs. 6	7 vs. 4	6 vs. 7
		1 vs. 6	9 vs. 12
			10 vs. 11
W13	1 vs. 4	10 vs. 8	1 vs. 3
	5 vs. 8	6 vs. 7	2 vs. 4
	2 vs. 3	3 vs. 1	5 vs. 7
	6 vs. 7	5 vs. 4	6 vs. 8
		9 vs. 2	9 vs. 11
			10 vs. 12
W14	2 vs. 1	7 vs. 9	1 vs. 2
	6 vs. 5	8 vs. 6	3 vs. 4
	4 vs. 3	2 vs. 5	5 vs. 6
	8 vs. 7	4 vs. 3	7 vs. 8
		1 vs. 10	9 vs. 10
			11 vs. 12
Wk15	1 vs. 5	10 vs. 4	Playoffs
	3 vs. 7	9 vs. 1	
	2 vs. 6	2 vs. 8	
	4 vs. 8	3 vs. 7	
		6 vs. 5	

See Lesson #6 for playoff options.

ORDER FORM

Postal Orders: Majestic Mountain Publishing,
PO Box 23338, Minneapolis, Mn 55423-9998

Email: KenK888@aol.com for Bulk order inquiries
Fantasyfootballlessons.com

Please send _____ Copies of Lessons:
7 Valuable lessons to make you a better Fantasy Football Player

Name: ________________________________

Address:______________________________

City:_________________________________

State:_______________ Zip:______________

Telephone:____________________________

Email address:_________________________

Fantasy Football: Lessons for $14.95 each
Sales Tax: Please add 6.5% for products shipped to Minnesota (Total of $15.92 includes tax)
Make check payable: Majestic Mountain Publishing
Add $4.00 for shipping and handling for 1 book, $2.00 for each additional book.

My check or money order for $________

Payment must accompany orders.